GROWING IN THE GOSPEL

Sound Doctrine for Daily Living

Volume 1

JASON VAN VLIET

LUCERNA
CRTS PUBLICATIONS

GROWING IN THE GOSPEL
Sound Doctrine for Daily Living

Lucerna Publications
110 West 27th Street
Hamilton, ON, Canada
L9C 5A1

Library and Archives Canada Cataloguing in Publication

Van Vliet, Jason, 1970-, author
Growing in the Gospel : sound doctrine for daily living / Jason Van Vliet.

Includes index.
ISBN 978-0-9948059-0-4 (paperback : v. 1).–ISBN 978-0-9948059-5-9 (ebook : v. 1)

1. Reformed Church–Doctrines. I. Title.

BX9422.3.V36 2016   230'.42   C2016-901836-9

To Curtis, Hannah, Ruth, Abigail
Philip, Joelle, and Jared

Our heritage from the LORD

Psalm 127:3

CONTENTS

PREFACE

Behind every book there is a story. That story usually involves a number of different people. Such is certainly the case with this book and its story.

It is hard to know precisely where to begin, but let me start with my years serving as a minister of the Word in the Vineyard Canadian Reformed Church in Lincoln, Ontario (1996-2004) and the Maranatha Canadian Reformed Church in Surrey, British Columbia (2004-2009). These congregations formed me in a profound way, probably more than both they and I realize, cultivating in me the conviction that sound doctrine impacts daily living in more ways than we can count. Now that I am busy putting the finishing touches to this book, it is clear to me that much of its content was already beginning to take shape as I had the privilege of serving these two congregations. To all my spiritual brothers and sisters in Vineyard and Maranatha, let me simply say, "Thank-you so much, and may our gracious God continue to bless you."

What began in the regular course of pastoral ministry definitely continued when our heavenly Father guided me to start teaching at the Canadian Reformed Theological Seminary in Hamilton, Ontario. The regular rigour of preparing lectures challenged me to dig deeper into the doctrines of grace that I had been preaching and teaching for years already. Added to that, theological students tend to come up with very good questions, yes, even challenging inquiries, which force a professor to hone his thinking and sharpen his formulations. To all my students at CRTS, both past and present, allow me to offer my sincere gratitude for the way in which you have helped me refine the material found in this book.

Yet even as the doctrines of grace are constantly being refined in our minds, some kind of catalyst is usually needed before a person sits down behind a keyboard and starts writing a book about them. In my case that catalyst came from the Asia Mission Board, an initiative jointly supervised by the Cloverdale and Langley Canadian Reformed Churches. They asked me to write a curriculum document that covered all the major doctrines of Scripture in a concise, organized, and accessible manner. With a desire to promote the spread of Christ's global kingdom, I agreed. It is my prayer that the curriculum document may assist the Asia Mission Board in its work for years to come. In addition, should the Lord bless this present publication with any financial gain, the profits will be earmarked for the work of the Asia Mission Board or similar mission-oriented initiatives.

As I worked on that curriculum project it slowly dawned on me that it could be adapted for profitable use in North America and elsewhere just as it will hopefully be beneficial on the Asian continent. This prompted me to take the entire project to a new level. Chapters had to be revamped. Connections to daily living needed a fresh look. Especially the question sections were largely re-written. More people also became involved: Dr. James Visscher read over the material with an eye for theological correctness and pastoral wisdom, Dr. William Helder and Mrs. Kristen Alkema meticulously ironed out the grammatical and syntactical wrinkles in my writing style, and Mr. Bernie Harsevoort and his team at Adverdea Digital Solutions used their expertise to design the book cover. Our seminary also allowed me some sabbatical time to focus on finalizing the project. To all of these kind and generous folk I extend my heartfelt appreciation. Any remaining weaknesses in this publication should be laid at my doorstep, not theirs.

Having said all of this, I have yet to mention the individuals who have made the greatest sacrifice during the writing and editing of this book: my dear wife, Janet, and our cherished children, to whom this book is dedicated. There is no way around the fact that writing a three-volume set such as *Growing in the Gospel* takes many hours. Throughout the entire process, Janet and our children were patient, understanding, and supportive. Words cannot fully express my gratitude to them, but this much I can say to my family: you are truly a gift from God to me, each and every one of you.

Finally, my greatest debt of gratitude is owed to our loving and triune God, Father, Son, and Holy Spirit. Plainly stated, if it were not for him this publication would not exist. The reason for this is simple: without God's gospel there would be nothing of substance for me to write about in a book like this. Every word on these pages ultimately traces its origin and value back to his Word. Thus, in a very real sense the story behind this book is his Story, the history of God's marvellous redemptive deeds, as revealed on the pages of Holy Scripture. May his Name and his kingdom be advanced through this publication.

Hamilton, Ontario
Christmas 2015

INTRODUCTION

A young Christian adult attending university is confused about truth. What is truth? How can anyone know with certainty who has the truth? Christians, Jews, Muslims, and Buddhists all have at least some good things to say. So how do we know who is right and who is wrong?

A women's Bible study group is struggling with the question of infant baptism. Does the Bible teach that newborn babies should be baptized? On the one hand, in Mark 16:16 they read, "Whoever believes and is baptized will be saved." On the other hand, in 1 Corinthians 1:16 they note that the entire household of Stephanas was baptized. This question of infant baptism is not just a theoretical debate for this study group. One lady grew up Baptist but later became Reformed. Another lady has a son who is thinking about leaving the Reformed church, joining a Baptist church, and being re-baptized. These sisters are not just talking about this issue; they are living it, in their hearts and in their families.

A five-year-old boy is dying from cancer. "Mom, what will happen to me when I die? What will it be like in heaven? Will I get to see Jesus?" With tear-stained cheeks and a lump in her throat, Mom wants to comfort her son. Yet what exactly should she say? Generally speaking, she knows what the Bible says about life after death but she is not entirely clear on all the details. How can she describe future glory in a way that provides solid reassurance to her suffering child?

In one way or the other each of these three scenarios, briefly sketched above, has to do with doctrine. This three-volume work is all about doctrine, which is simply another way of referring to the teachings of Scripture. It all begins in the first volume with learning about the God who reveals himself and it ends in the last volume with a look at the return of Jesus Christ, who will bring us into final glory. Between these two bookends nearly every major doctrine of the Christian faith receives at least some attention.

At the same time, these volumes are not *merely* about doctrine. They are also about life, daily life as it is experienced by dads, moms, singles, and teenagers, including people who are healthy, sick, happy, and distressed—in short, real people like you and me who are living real lives in a really broken world. Some might feel it is a stretch to pull these two realms—detailed doctrine and daily life—together into one publication. Would it not be better, and much tidier, to focus on all the doctrines of Scripture in one book, and then perhaps write another book that seeks to guide Christians in how they should live godly lives in the midst of an ungodly world? Such an approach is possible, and it has been done. Yet it also has a significant drawback. Life is not so neatly organized into separate cubby-holes: doctrine in one compartment and daily activities in the next one over. In fact, life *should not* be compartmentalized in any such way. To detach doctrine from daily living is not only unnatural but also unscriptural. For example, in his letter to the Ephesians the apostle Paul moves from the deep doctrine of predestination (1:3-5) to the daily practice of prayer (1:15-23), from the truth of total depravity (2:1-3) to the right way of living together with Christians who come from different ethnic backgrounds (2:11-22). Remarkably, his transitions between teaching and practice are virtually seamless. So if doctrine and daily life were one integrated unit for the inspired apostle, then they should be nothing less for us.

Each volume of *Growing in the Gospel* aims to integrate what we believe from Scripture with how we deal with the issues that arise in the course of our regular work and studies. The word order in the previous sentence is important: God's Word comes first, as the starting point and underlying foundation, and then we take his Word and apply it in our lives. This order is entirely logical. Since God is infinite, eternal, and entirely perfect and, by contrast, we are finite, fallen, and fallible, it stands to reason that *he* should always have priority over *us*. In practice, though, it is much harder to keep that order straight. All too often we attempt to create God in our own image. We make his Word say whatever keeps our lives most comfortable and convenient. In this publication we are going to fight against that temptation. The constant goal will be to let God speak first, and after we have listened carefully we will do our best to apply his truth wisely. It will not be easy. Prayer will be necessary.

WHO WILL BENEFIT FROM THIS BOOK?

Any author is inclined to think that everyone will benefit from whatever he has written. Reality teaches us to have more modest expectations. As the title already suggests, *Growing in the Gospel* is for Christians in whom the seed of new life, "the living and abiding Word of God" (1 Pet 1:23), has been planted, taken root, and begun to grow. Indeed, they have already matured quite a bit in the faith, but there is always more growing to be done. For most people physical growth stops at some point during their teenage years. For every child of God spiritual growth never stops, no matter how old you may be.

To put things plainly, this book is not for new converts or young children who are learning the rudiments of the faith. If you are looking for a basic introduction to Christian doctrine, you will need to look elsewhere. However, if you are a believer who is already familiar with the essentials of the gospel, and you are looking to take the next solid step forward in your understanding of the truth of Scripture, then it is my prayer that you will be able to profit from these pages.

Some examples may help to clarify matters. Perhaps you are a member of a Bible study group. You have studied various books of the Bible, chapter by chapter, even verse by verse. Yet as you study various parts of the Bible you keep running into certain doctrinal questions: How do we fit together the wrath and the love of God? How can God be sovereign over sinners without being guilty of sin himself? If Jesus Christ is human, did he still have to learn things, or did he know everything in advance because he is also divine? What exactly is speaking in tongues, and should we still be able to do it today? All these are important questions, but in Bible study groups there is often precious little time to dig into what the whole Bible says about them because we want to move on and finish the chapter before the evening is over. *Growing in the Gospel* provides Bible study groups with the opportunity to zero in on all the major doctrines, one by one, and explore the biblical breadth of what the Lord teaches us about each. This, in turn, will equip God's people to understand specific passages of the Bible more fully and accurately.

Then again, you may be a young adult who has spent a good number of years learning the basics of the faith in a catechism class or some other kind of Christian education environment. You have learned a lot, but now that you are finished with those classes you are wondering what comes next. Yes, you graduate from high school and then it is done. But you never graduate from the school of faith. So what is the next step in your ongoing spiritual growth? This is where *Growing in the Gospel* fits in. It takes you further into the doctrines of grace but, to be sure, we will also review the basics along the way. The goal is to dig deeper but remain accessible.

Growing in the Gospel may also serve office-bearers who want a concise overview of key doctrines. Men who are ordained as elders or deacons often feel inadequate. They have a sincere desire to serve the Lord in this special capacity, but they are not entirely convinced they know everything that they should know in order to lead God's flock in the paths of truth and holiness. Inevitably, while visiting members of the congregation, doctrinal matters will come up, sometimes at the most unpredictable moments and in the most unexpected manner. On such occasions office-bearers often think to themselves, "Why didn't I pay more attention back in catechism class? And, yes, I remember our minister preached on this topic not so long ago, but I can't quite recall exactly what he said and especially how he put it all together." If office-bearers, and particularly elders, ought to be "able to teach" (1 Tim 3:2), then we also need to enable them to teach. Under the Lord's blessing, office-bearers can use *Growing in the Gospel* as a doctrinal quick reference guide, helping them to do the vital work that our God has ordained them to do.

Beyond that, these volumes can also simply be read for personal edification. As mentioned earlier, the doctrinal truths that we are about to explore ought never to be disconnected from daily life. As God's children we constantly need spiritual nourishment and reinvigoration as well as correction and redirection. In our families, at our workplaces, with our neighbours, and from our own minds, questions come up and issues arise. Not all of them are easy to deal with. Clear doctrinal light shed on murky, messy situations is something we all look for—and rightly so, we all need it. To that end, you can read these volumes systematically, chapter after chapter, or by turning to the particular chapter that best applies to the present reality of your daily life.

WHAT TO EXPECT FROM THIS BOOK

There are four features of *Growing in the Gospel* that should stand out as you read each chapter. In the first place, it is *biblical*. On the one hand, this should be a given for any Christian publication. On the other hand, it is more challenging to achieve than it may first seem. It is easy to drift off into the unsettled waves of human opinion rather than remaining firmly attached to the anchor of divine revelation. This is why you will see so many references to Scripture throughout each chapter. They are there just as much for me, the author, as they are for you, the reader. It is a simple way of keeping all of us grounded in the Word.

God's Word contains two testaments or covenants: an old and a new. In doctrinal studies the vast majority of Scripture references usually come from the New Testament. To a degree that is understandable, but to an even larger degree that is impoverishing. There is so much rich, vibrant, and concrete doctrinal instruction in the Old Testament. For this reason we have made a conscious effort not to skip immediately into the New Testament, but to explore first what treasures are concealed in the Old before turning to what is revealed in the New.

Secondly, this is a *confessional* publication, and unabashedly so. Although confessions are not inspired, they are time-honoured and ecclesiastically adopted summaries of God's Holy Word. As such they are a valuable aid in seeing the forest for the trees in doctrinal matters. To be more specific, ample use is made of the ecumenical creeds—the Apostles' Creed, the Nicene Creed, and the Athanasian Creed—as well as the continental Reformed confessions, more commonly known as the Three Forms of Unity—the Belgic Confession, the Heidelberg Catechism, and the Canons of Dort. The Westminster Confession and Catechisms will also be referenced from time to time, but not frequently. The simple reason for this is that the present author grew up with the Three Forms of Unity and therefore finds them most familiar. If you because of your ecclesiastical background make greater use of the Westminster Standards, let me recommend the following book: *Reformed Confessions Harmonized*, edited by Joel Beeke and Sinclair Ferguson (Baker Books, 1999). In that handy volume you will find the Three Forms of Unity and the Westminster Standards printed in parallel columns and you can easily cross-reference from one set of Reformed confessions to the other.

The Three Forms of Unity will be referenced in the following way:

- *LD 7, Q&A 21* means Lord's Day 7, Question and Answer 21 of the Heidelberg Catechism;

- *BC 25* is an abbreviation for Belgic Confession Article 25;

- *CoD 3/4.4* is a reference to the Canons of Dort, Chapter 3/4, Article 4.

Thirdly, this three-volume set is organized in a *systematic* manner. Hopefully every book is organized systematically, but in this case *systematic* has a particular meaning. It refers to the manner in which doctrinal topics are commonly arranged in systematic theologies. Traditionally yet not exclusively, systematic theologies work through the full-range of doctrinal questions under six consecutive headings: the doctrine of God (theology proper), the doctrine of man (anthropology), the doctrine of Christ (Christology), the doctrine of salvation (soteriology), the doctrine of the church (ecclesiology), and the doctrine of the last things (eschatology). A quick scan of the table of contents will reveal that *Growing in the Gospel* uses this time-honoured division. Yet it does not do so rigorously. The discipline of biblical theology, as distinguished from systematic theology, aims to describe how God has revealed his truth throughout redemptive history "at many times and in many ways" (Heb 1:1). The manner in which the Holy Spirit slowly unfolds the gospel from the time of the patriarchs, through the era of the prophets, and on into the age of the apostles is a beautiful thing to behold. From time to time we will pause to take a glimpse at that Spirit-breathed unravelling.

Finally, *Growing in the Gospel* endeavours to be *practical*. Nearly every chapter begins with a real life situation. Sometimes it is a fictional anecdote; other times it is an historical account. Some chapters begin with a series of challenging questions; others start with a description of circumstances that we can all identify with. Yet whatever approach is taken, the point of departure is always the same: not up in the theoretical clouds but down here on the *terra firma* of daily life. Typically the chapter will then work its way through various passages from Scripture and confessional references which pertain to the specific doctrine that is being explored. Along the way, various insights from church history may be added and comparisons to other world religions may be made. Here and there the doctrine is briefly connected to our daily life. The end of the chapter, though, much like the beginning, brings our daily life to the fore again. This is especially so in the questions that you will find there. They are presented in two sections: *Questions for Understanding* and *Questions for Further Discussion*. Particularly the latter group challenges us to take the truths that God reveals to us and apply them in the nitty-gritty of our weekly work and worship. The challenge will not always be easy to meet, but the discussion that results will hopefully be edifying and enlightening.

HOW TO USE THIS BOOK

This publication is primarily designed to be used as a guide for adult Bible study groups, whether they are comprised of younger adults, older persons, or a healthy mix of both. Each member of the study group is encouraged to read in advance the chapter that has been scheduled for discussion. Toward the end of each chapter, before the question section, there is also a suggested reading from Scripture. This includes one or two main passages that are connected with the topic at hand. Reading this passage in advance will certainly keep everyone's pre-meeting preparations grounded in God's Word. Undoubtedly there are many more passages that are important; a good number of them are mentioned within the chapter. As time allows, each member of the group can consult at least some of these Scripture passages as well. In addition, looking up some of the confessional references will be a helpful.

When the Bible study group gathers together, the suggested reading can be used at the beginning of the meeting, although this is not necessary. Discussion can then begin using the *Questions for Understanding*. This will ensure that everyone in the group comprehends the essential truths associated with the doctrine being discussed. It is always best to have a solid grasp of the basics before delving into the necessary task of applying these truths to our lives. All things being well, a study group should be able to move through the *Questions for Understanding* in a fairly time-efficient manner. This should leave ample time to discuss the more challenging questions found in the next section: *Questions for Further Discussion*. It may not be possible to finish dealing with all of these questions in one session. The group may decide to carry the discussion over into the next meeting, or it may also prefer to leave some questions for personal reflection rather than communal discussion.

Alternately, this material could be used in a classroom or guided study setting as well. In this case the pastor, elder, or group leader would guide everyone in the class through the material, using the Scripture passages and confessional references to expand on what is presented in the chapter. After the session, the class could be asked to complete the questions on their own time. At the next meeting the teacher could review some of the answers with everyone, giving further explanation and guidance as needed.

Concerning confessional references, readers who are unfamiliar with the Three Forms of Unity may find them online in various locations. Although there are many more, I can point you to two sources: www.canrc.org (look under the menu item "Doctrine") and www.heidelberg-catechism.com.

As alluded to earlier, this publication can also be used as a doctrinal quick reference guide for anyone looking to brush up on a certain doctrine and delve deeper into the multifaceted treasures of the gospel. The index in the back includes references to all three volumes. In this way, regardless of which volume you may have in your hand, you will always know which one you need to find the topic that you are interested in.

In conclusion, our Lord Jesus Christ compared the Word of the gospel to seeds that can produce an abundant harvest when they fall into fertile soil that is being carefully cultivated by God's Spirit and constantly nourished by the refreshing rains and radiant sunshine of God's grace (Mark 4:1-9). It is my prayer that in some small way the following chapters can help God's people to continue growing in the gospel so that they might yield thirtyfold, sixtyfold, and even a hundredfold—all to the further glory of our Redeemer's great name.

CHAPTER 1.

STUDYING DOCTRINE

Theology. Doctrine. Dogma. To most people these words sound heavy. They make people think of scholars who talk about the Christian faith in an unnecessarily complicated way, using big words and complex concepts. To be sure, pastors should study theology, and seminary students love to dive into the intricacies of doctrine. But does the man who fixes cars from nine to five need to do the same? Or what shall we say about the mom who is working all hours of the day and evening just to stay on top of all the hustle and bustle in her busy family? Do average Joes and Janes need to study doctrine?

Before we answer that particular question, we need to explore another matter. Does studying doctrine tend to drain the joy out of Christian souls? At the seminary where I work, my main task is to teach the courses in doctrine, or dogmatics, as it is sometimes called. I still remember the day that I tried to explain this to a librarian in one of our local public libraries. With one eyebrow raised high above her reading glasses, she asked, "So, you are a professor of dogmatics?" "Yes," I replied, "that's correct." To which she responded, "So you're actually telling me that you teach people to be stubborn and narrow-minded?"

That humorous conversation with the librarian was a humbling experience, I must admit. At the same time, it taught me something. Many people, both outside and inside the church, associate negative things with words like *doctrine* or *dogmatics*. Or, even if these words do not have overly negative connotations for them, they certainly do not radiate overwhelmingly positive vibes. If Christians want to renew their zeal, they usually want to sing a solid, upbeat hymn or have a good heart-to-heart with a fellow believer about the challenge of living as God's children in a decidedly secular society. Most of the time, though, doctrine and joy are not found together in the same sentence.

All of this leads us to ask yet a third question. What is the content of our joy? Or, to put it in different words, *why* should we be joyful? Most Christians would point to Christ as the source of their joy, and rightly so. The apostle Paul urges us to "rejoice in the Lord always" (Phil 4:4), and in that context he is referring specifically to the "Lord Jesus Christ" (Phil 3:20). But there is so much to learn about Christ and his eternal Father and the Holy Spirit. The same apostle once prayed that members of the church might grasp, together with all their fellow Christians, how wide and long and high and deep is the love of Christ (Eph 3:18). When we study doctrine, that is really what we are learning. In an organized way, we are busy exploring the width and the length, as well as the height and the depth, of the love of Christ, which is revealed to us in the holy gospel.

So, now we are set to answer our initial questions. First, do average Joes and Janes need to study doctrine? Yes, because then they will know the love of Christ in deeper detail. Second, does studying doctrine rob Christians of their joy? Quite the opposite. To know the love of Christ better is to grow in joy. Third, what is the content of our joy? It is the gospel of salvation in Jesus Christ. When we study doctrine, that is precisely what we are learning. *Growing in the Gospel*: this is not only the title of this book but also the blessed benefit of studying doctrine.

WHAT EXACTLY IS DOCTRINE?

In order to define doctrine more precisely, we need to look at two things. First, we need to look more broadly at how studying doctrine relates to other ways of studying the Bible. Second, it is helpful to zero in on that one word *doctrine* and see what it means.

When Christians study the Bible in an organized way, they usually focus on one book of the Bible for a length of time. They may, for example, study the prophecy of Malachi or the gospel of Matthew. Also in personal devotions, people tend to read certain sections of Scripture, at one time working through the books of Moses while at another time going through the letters of Paul. As we study parts of the Bible we are usually looking for certain themes as well. We may ask questions such as: what does Leviticus teach us about sacrifice, or what does Ephesians teach us about the church? But what if we want to know what the entire Bible teaches on a certain topic? For example, what does the whole Bible teach about how people are converted to faith? Or what does the Bible teach about the return of Jesus Christ? When we start asking questions like that, we are studying doctrine. This approach to studying the truth of Scripture is also called *systematic theology* or *dogmatics*.

Of course, asking what the entire Bible teaches on various topics runs the risk of leading to some very long answers. After all, the Bible is a big book. There is a lot to say about each topic the Lord addresses in his Word. However, during the history of the church God has blessed us with some helpful summaries of doctrinal truth. These summaries are generally called *creeds* if they happen to be quite short, or confessions if they are a little longer. The ecumenical creeds are the Apostles' Creed, the Nicene Creed, and Athanasian Creed. They originate from the early centuries of the Christian church but are still recognized and used throughout the world today. A number of valuable confessions as well as teaching summaries called *catechisms* were produced in the Reformation in the sixteenth century. In this book we will refer to the Belgic Confession (1561), the Heidelberg Catechism (1563), and the Canons of Dort (1618–19). Together these three confessions are known as the Three Forms of Unity.

Technically speaking, the study of creeds in a concentrated manner is also called *symbolics*. This term goes back to the early church, when people sometimes referred to creeds as symbols of the faith. Yet whatever term we use, whether creed, confession, catechism, or symbol, they are all simply summaries of what God teaches us in the Bible. They do not have the same level of authority as God's inspired Word. They also do not add anything to God's Word. We respect them, however, because they have proved to be faithful summaries of Scripture. As mentioned earlier, the apostle Paul says that we should learn about the extent of Christ's love for us together "with all the saints" (Eph 3:18), also those saints who lived in previous centuries. Confessions help us in doing so. Therefore we gladly and gratefully make use of them when we study doctrine.

Yet someone will surely ask, "Does all of this doctrine help us any in our daily life?" People tend to be practical. They want to know how to improve their prayer life. They want advice on how to keep their marriage strong. This desire to apply faith in the nitty-gritty of life is entirely scriptural (Jas 2:17). At the same time, though, sound doctrine and daily life are not two separate compartments, at least not in the apostle Paul's mind. No sooner does he give us a symphony of deep doctrinal truths in the first half of Ephesians 1 than he immediately launches into a paragraph on prayer in the second half of the same chapter. Similarly, his teaching on Christian marriage is all wrapped up together with his doctrine of the church, to the point that he even sums up his instructions to husbands and wives by saying, "This mystery is profound, and I am saying that it refers to Christ and the church" (Eph 5:32). Sound doctrine therefore finds its proper goal in holy living, and holy living is necessarily built on the solid foundation of sound doctrine. You cannot have one without the other.

Next we need to zero in for a moment on that one word *doctrine*. It comes from a Latin word that simply means *teaching*. Teaching is what our Saviour Jesus Christ focused on after he was anointed by the Holy Spirit. He walked throughout Galilee and Judea teaching in the synagogues and temple courts (Matt 4:23; 26:55). To be sure, he also did miraculous healings that attracted crowds from near and far (Matt 4:25). But when those crowds gathered, by the hundreds and even thousands, our Saviour seized those opportunities to teach (Matt 5:1–2). Also, just before he returned to his Father in heaven, Jesus Christ charged his disciples to concentrate on doctrine when he said, "Go therefore and make *disciples* [that is, students] of all nations, baptizing them in the name of the Father and of the Son and of the Holy Spirit, *teaching* [there is the word again] them to observe all that I have commanded you" (Matt 28:19–20). Since our ascended Lord concentrated so much of his time on teaching doctrine while he was here on this earth, we, as his pupils, will gladly learn everything he has to teach us.

While we are on the topic of defining words more carefully, it is good to be more precise about another term that we have already encountered: *dogma*. You remember the librarian who was perplexed as to why a professor of dogmatics would teach people to be narrow-minded. This may come as a surprise to some, but in the Bible the word *dogma* has more to do with being broad-minded than narrow-minded. Shortly after our Lord ascended into heaven, the church wrestled with questions such as, "Do those who believe in Christ have to follow the Old Testament laws concerning clean and unclean food?" Eventually the apostles and the elders gathered in Jerusalem. Together they discussed this issue carefully and took some official decisions. All of this is recorded in Acts 15.

The leaders in the church took the time to come together because they did not want such sensitive questions to be answered merely on the basis of one man's personal opinion. They sought after a much broader consensus. Not only that, but when they had reached a consensus, they wrote up a letter explaining matters and sent a delegation to communicate the decisions to the churches (Acts 15:22–35). In the original Greek language these communal decisions are called *dogmas*. In Acts 16:4 we read: "As they went on their way through the cities, they delivered to them for observance the *decisions* that had been reached by the apostles and elders who were in Jerusalem." So, in the Bible the word *dogma* refers to explanations of God's truth, revealed in Scripture and agreed upon in the church—not just narrow personal opinions. Moreover, the Holy Spirit informs us that these dogmas certainly did not dampen the joy of the Christians but, instead, strengthened them in their faith (Acts 16:5).

There is always a temptation for different individuals or groups of people to run off in different directions: one teaching one thing and the other teaching a different thing. But since we serve *one* Lord, who has given us *one* Bible, we must resist the temptation to allow all kinds of different contradictory teachings in the church. Patiently, yet persistently, the church needs to aim for more and more unity and consistency in doctrine.

WHERE DOES DOCTRINE COME FROM?

If we are going to grow in our understanding of sound doctrine, we need to ask, "Where do we go to find it?" In short, the answer is that we must go to God's Word, the Bible. In 2 Timothy 3:16 the apostle Paul writes, "All Scripture is breathed out by God and profitable for teaching, for reproof, for correction, and for training in righteousness." It is worthwhile noting that of all the things for which Scripture is useful, teaching is the first one on the list.

Now most Christians will agree that we must turn to Scripture as the source of our teaching. But will Scripture be the sole source of our doctrine, or will there be other sources in addition to Scripture? That is a very important question.

The Roman Catholic Church promotes two sources: the written Scripture *plus* the oral tradition. One of its major ecclesiastical assemblies, the Council of Trent (1545–63), even declared officially that Rome accepts both Scripture and tradition with "an equal affection of piety and reverence."[1] In 1965, at another large ecclesiastical gathering called Vatican II, the Roman Catholic Church reaffirmed this teaching.

Then there are also those who build their theology on the twin pillars of divine revelation *plus* human philosophy. You can understand how this might happen. Philosophy sometimes deals with questions about God. Who is God? How can we know about him? Can we prove that God really exists? Philosophy also deals with ethical questions. How do we determine what is morally right and wrong? Is there such a thing as the

---

1. Council of Trent, Session IV, April 8, 1546, "Decree concerning the canonical Scriptures."

highest good? Since Scripture and philosophy both address some similar questions, it is easy to see how people might combine them as they seek for answers. We must remember, however, that philosophy comes from below, from human reason, while Scripture comes from above, from God. In this way they are fundamentally different (1 Cor 1:20–25; 2:1–16). (We will come back to this in more detail in chapter 4.)

But even if we are not particularly interested in the decrees of Rome or the deliberations of philosophers, most of us are still tempted to use a more subtle two-source approach in theology. For lack of a better term, this approach might be called Scripture *plus* my desires. The apostle Paul warns against this in 2 Timothy 4:1–5 when he speaks about itching ears (v. 3). Different people have different desires. Sick people want to be healed. Poor people want to be richer. Sad people want to be happy. Lonely people want to be popular. The desires may be different, but one thing is the same: desire is an internal force to be reckoned with. It is like an itching ear that we simply *must* scratch. Without a doubt there are more than enough teachers, even those who use the name of Christ, who are very skilled at scratching people's itching ears. They know just what to say and how to say it. If people are itching to be rich, these teachers will tell them how they can get rich. If someone is itching to be healed, these teachers will have a cure.

Be careful, warns the apostle Paul. Why are people running to these teachers? Is it simply because they are skilful at scratching an itch? What about the doctrine, that is, the teaching, of these teachers? Is it sound? This is what the apostle Paul draws to our attention. There are teachers who will turn people's ears away from the truth and fill them with empty myths and false hopes instead (2 Tim 4:4). However, the church that is faithful must focus on "sound teaching" (2 Tim 4:3).

Summing up, there are people who add human tradition to God's holy Word. Others attach human reason. Still others include their own desires as a source of their theology. However, when we study doctrine, it must not be Scripture *plus* anything else. Why? Simply put, because neither tradition, nor philosophy, nor our own desires ever redeemed anyone from a single sin, let alone from slavery to sin. The LORD, he *alone,* is our Redeemer (Isa 44:6). Therefore he *alone* is the one who reveals the way of salvation, and Scripture *alone* is God-breathed, that is, inspired (2 Tim 3:16). Therefore the one source of sound doctrine is the God-breathed Scripture—*all* of it!

WHY BOTHER WITH DOCTRINE?

Even if we use the correct source for our theology, there is still the matter of motivation. Is sound doctrine something that stirs up our enthusiasm?

The apostle Paul was clearly passionate about teaching the gospel correctly. When the church at Galatia was beginning to embrace unsound doctrine, he was deeply concerned and exclaimed, "I am astonished that you are so quickly deserting him who called you in the grace of Christ and are turning to a different gospel—not that there is another one" (Gal 1:6–7). Later he added, "O foolish Galatians! Who has bewitched you?" (3:1). Those are hardly indifferent or merely academic words.

Yet why is the Apostle Paul so passionate about having *correct* teaching in the churches? In the first place, as he writes in 1 Timothy 6:3, sound doctrine includes "the sound words of our Lord Jesus Christ." In other words, sound doctrine is not ours to do with as we please. It belongs to, and it focuses upon, Jesus Christ, who is our majestic and merciful Saviour. As his servants we are responsible for taking good care of that precious doctrine. If we are not passionate about protecting the pure teachings of our Master, then we are wicked and lazy servants (Matt 25:26).

There is another aspect of sound doctrine that should prevent us from ever becoming lethargic about it. The apostle Paul reminds Timothy that "sound doctrine" is something that conforms to "the gospel of the glory of the blessed God" (1 Tim 1:10–11). This glorious gospel is the "power of God for salvation to everyone who believes" (Rom 1:16). This gospel announces that in Christ we are freed from slavery to sin and Satan! And therefore the apostle writes: "Do not submit again to a yoke of slavery"

(Gal 5:1); do not let yourselves be trapped by "words of eloquent wisdom" that empty the cross of Christ of its power (1 Cor 1:17).

In short, we should be passionate about learning sound doctrine because without it we will quickly be re-enslaved under the power of sin and the deceit of Satan. With every fibre of our being we want to avoid that misery.

HOW SHOULD WE STUDY DOCTRINE?

To begin with, all teachers and students of doctrine should be filled with humility. After the LORD redeemed his people from Egypt and brought them into the Promised Land, they began to turn away from him when their hearts became proud (Deut 8:14). Furthermore, it is striking how often Scripture associates false teachers with conceit, pride, and boastful words (Gal 6:13; 1 Tim 6:3–4; 2 Pet 2:18; Jude 16; Rev 13:5). Since we are servants of our Lord Jesus Christ, we must conduct ourselves in exactly that way, as servants who have no basis for boasting in themselves.

Indeed, instead of boasting, servants should focus on serving. If we grow in the doctrine of the gospel ourselves, we can help dish up its nourishing truths to others. Now you may wonder why we are comparing doctrine to food. The answer is this. In his letters to Timothy and Titus, the apostle Paul speaks about sound doctrine or instruction no fewer than eight times (1 Tim 1:10; 6:3; 2 Tim 1:13; 4:3; Titus 1:9; 1:13; 2:1, 8). The word *sound* has to do with being healthy. When we eat and digest the food of healthy doctrinal teaching, we ourselves will be spiritually healthy and strong. If, however, we eat spiritual food that is partially or completely rotten due to false teachings, we will become spiritually sick and weak.

Healthy food must also be properly prepared. The spiritual menu must be considered carefully. Over the long term, meals must be balanced so that the church, which is God's household (1 Tim 3:15), will be well nourished. If there is too much emphasis on God the Spirit and not enough on God the Son, or the other way around, then the family of God will be malnourished. If there is too much emphasis on how Christians should live and not enough on what Christ has done for us, or the other way around, God's household will not receive all the nutrients that it needs.

Finally, thinking about doctrine as nourishment helps us see how it is connected to daily living. After all, why do we eat? We eat to gain strength and energy to live and work. Likewise we digest healthy doctrine so that we can stand up, be active, and live holy lives (1 Tim 1:10; 6:3; Titus 1:8; 2:1, 8).

WHAT IS THE GOAL?

In any given task it is necessary to keep an eye firmly focused on the end goal. Those who do not know their final destination tend to get lost somewhere along the way.

This is also true in studying doctrine. Our goal is not to build a big and impressive intellectual palace to which the admiring crowds will flock. In fact, in the end it is not about a building that we construct; it is about a Bride whom Christ has chosen in his love (Eph 5:25–26, 29–30). Right now, the beauty of Christ's bride, the church, is not always so obvious. She still has many blemishes, that is, sins. She still has to mature, that is, to grow in understanding. But one day the church will appear as the Bride of Christ, beautifully dressed for her husband (Rev 21:2). Learning sound doctrine is all part of preparing Christ's Bride for her wedding day. We need to keep that goal in our minds and in our hearts.

Still, there is an even greater goal than that. Since Christ "has ransomed us, body and soul, from all our sins, not with silver or gold but with His precious blood" (LD 13), we call him our Lord, that is, our majestic and merciful Master. Therefore we, as his redeemed servants, strive to remain faithful to him in everything. In this way the Son who redeemed us, the Spirit who sanctifies us, and the Father who created us will receive all the honour and glory. Ultimately, *that* is what studying sound doctrine is all about.

Suggested Readings: 1 Corinthians 2; 2 Timothy 4:1–5

1. What does the word *doctrine* mean? What does the word *dogma* mean? Read Titus 2:1–10, which gives a description of "sound doctrine" applied in the lives of different age groups and genders. Why would we associate most of the things mentioned in that passage with ethics rather than with doctrine? When and how did the meaning of the word *doctrine* change to exclude, generally speaking, matters pertaining to a godly lifestyle? How can we recapture the full biblical sense of this term?

2. Some people build their theology on a two-fold foundation. Give some examples from this chapter showing how this happens. Can you think of one or two more, beyond those mentioned in this chapter?

3. Why was the apostle Paul so passionate about making sure churches did not deviate from sound doctrine?

4. What are the two main goals in studying doctrine?

QUESTIONS FOR FURTHER DISCUSSION

1. If a fellow Christian is not interested in studying doctrine carefully, how could you motivate such a person to become more enthusiastic about digging deeper into the truths of the gospel?

2. At other times the problem is not so much that Christians are uninterested in doctrine but rather that they feel intimidated by it since there are some complex issues at stake. For example, studying the doctrine of the Trinity can quickly go over people's heads. What can we do to reduce the intimidation factor? How does a document like the Heidelberg Catechism help in this? (See LD 8 concerning Trinity.) What other aids can you think of?

3. In your own experience in the church, have you noticed examples of unbalanced doctrinal teaching? Which imbalances have you noticed? How could you work in a positive and Christian manner in order to improve the teaching being given and received?

4. Since doctrine is ultimately meant to lead us to doxology, or

praising God, how can this be brought into sharper focus both in your own personal life and within God's household as a whole?

CHAPTER 2.

THE GOD WHO REVEALS HIMSELF

Jane lived in Smalltown, Nebraska. She appreciated the sense of community. Many people in town knew each other and helped each other out. Lately, though, life in Smalltown was not as harmonious as it could be. The local newspaper, *The Smalltown Gazette*, published several editorials criticizing the town's long-time mayor, Ed Johnson. The *Gazette* accused him of becoming callous and uncompassionate. It cited various examples of how the mayor had ignored the needs of the citizens and charged ahead in his own domineering way.

Never one to pay much attention to politics, Jane mostly ignored the gossip swirling around the mayor. At least, she did so until her friend Samantha came over one evening all in a fluster. Samantha owned the local flower shop in town and had spent the better part of two months trying to resolve a property tax issue with the town. Earlier that day Samantha had met the mayor walking on the street and had tried to ask him about her difficulty. Sadly, Mr. Johnson had brushed off Samantha's polite request with a brusque response: "Sorry, I'm busy. Please contact the town clerk." Apparently the *Gazette* was right, and Jane began to take a rather dim view of her local governing official.

That dim view brightened rather suddenly, though, when Jane went to the hospital to visit her ten-year-old niece, who was suffering from cancer. The hospital was a sixty-minute drive away in Largeville. Much to her surprise, as she was leaving the hospital she met Mayor Johnson in the lobby. She greeted him and asked him what he was doing in the Largeville hospital. He said that he was visiting his wife, who was going through chemotherapy. Without further prompting he went on to explain that his wife was a very private individual and did not want the media to know about her sickness. Finding common ground in their concern about ailing loved ones, Jane and the mayor had a good long talk, in which he confided how stressful it was, trying on the one hand to be there for his wife, and yet on the other hand keeping up with all his regular duties in Smalltown. Shielding the matter from the media, out of respect for his wife's need for privacy, only made the situation more challenging. Once the mayor revealed what was all going on in his life, Jane realized the *Gazette* was most certainly wrong.

Obviously the anecdote above is fiction. But most of us can recall a real-life example of how we received a completely different impression of someone after we actually listened to him explain his own situation. Much the same is true about God. Many people have heard things about God, or gathered ideas about God by observing Christians. Some of those impressions may be correct; others, like the *Gazette* editorial, may be completely off the mark.

Thankfully, God does reveal who he really is. At the beginning of the book of Hebrews we read, "Long ago, at many times and in many ways, God spoke to our fathers by the prophets, but in these last days he has spoken to us by his Son, whom he appointed the heir of all things, through whom also he created the world" (1:1–2). These words elo-quently express the main theme of this chapter. God speaks, and he speaks to us. Many people speculate about God. But who is to say which person is right and which one is wrong? However, as the Holy Spirit makes clear in Hebrews, what really counts is not what we say about God but rather what he has said to us.

THE LIGHT OF NATURE

Some people know the Bible and believe what it says. Other people know about the Bible, but they reject what it says. Still others do not know the Bible at all. Yet virtually everyone has some idea there is a God, or Higher Being, or Supreme Intelligence. Some people work hard intellectually to suppress this idea. In fact, some people work at it so hard that they manage to convince themselves that there is no God. If, however, they are honest enough to admit it, most people have an idea in their mind that there is such a thing as a divine being.

Where does that idea come from? Romans 1:18–20 speaks about this. For example, in verse 20 we read, "For his invisible attributes, namely, his eternal power and divine nature, have been clearly perceived, ever since the creation of the world, in the things that have been made. So they are without excuse." Sometimes the general idea that God exists is called the seed of religion.

Closely related to this is the fact that all human beings also have a conscience. The conscience is that voice inside of us which says, "What you are planning to do is completely wrong!" Or, if our conscience is clear, that voice says, "Don't worry about what other people say. You know that you're doing this for the right reason." Now, consciences are not always consistent. The inner voice says different things to different people at different times. Still, generally speaking, human beings know what it means to have their conscience speaking to them. In Romans 2:14–15 the apostle Paul also deals with how the conscience functions. There he describes its role in this way: "They show that the work of the law is written on their hearts, while their conscience also bears witness, and their conflicting thoughts accuse or even excuse them."

The Canons of Dort have summarized the Bible's teaching about the seed of religion and the conscience, using the phrase *the light of nature* to cover both aspects (3/4.4). You will notice that the Canons acknowledge that the light of nature exists, but they also indicate that it is not enough to give people a saving knowledge of God. In other words, the light of nature may give someone a notion about God, but it does not give salvation in Christ. This is in line with what the apostle Paul writes in Romans 1:20. The seed of religion does not lead people to salvation; instead, it leaves them "without excuse."

Understanding the light of nature also helps us explain the remarkably good deeds that unbelievers will do, at times even putting Christians to shame. There are many examples of people who refuse to acknowledge Jesus Christ and yet donate large sums of money or spend countless hours volunteering to do arduous and thankless work. When confronted with these impressive humanitarian efforts, Christians sometimes wonder whether we perhaps overemphasize the effects of sin. Is the human race inherently good after all? No, it is not, but God does speak to us about the light of nature. He is also the one who explains the power of the conscience that leads people to help others. The light of nature does not, however, reveal the full truth of who God is, and it certainly does not guide people down the path of salvation.

PRAGMATIC THEOLOGY

If you speak to a theologian and ask him what he thinks about pragmatic theology, he may well raise his eyebrow and ask, "What exactly do you mean by pragmatic theology?" In fact, it is not an official technical term. It is simply a term that we will be using for lack of a better one.

Pragmatic theology starts with the practical situations of daily life. For example, Christians also become sick, sometimes seriously sick. Just like other people, they would like to become healthy again. There are those who therefore teach, in the name of Christ, that if a Christian believes firmly enough and prays earnestly enough, he will certainly be healed. This is preaching that appears to connect with people concretely in their daily struggles. Moreover, preachers may even point to a passage like James 5:15 to support such a teaching: "And the prayer of faith will save the one who is sick, and the Lord will raise him up."

But there is one major problem with pragmatic theology. With this approach, God's revelation tends to come at the end rather than at the beginning. For when we start with what God says to us, we quickly realize that it is not as simple as quoting James 5:15 and then announcing that you will be healed if you pray hard enough. The apostle Paul certainly believed in the Lord, and he prayed frequently and earnestly (1 Thess 1:2–3). The apostle also had some kind of illness or physical handicap. He called it the thorn in his flesh (2 Cor 12:7). In prayer he pleaded with the Lord to take it away, but the Lord said, "No." And he added, "My grace is sufficient for you" (2 Cor 12:8–9). Also the young preacher Timothy was a faithful servant of the Lord; however, he was frequently sick (1 Tim 5:23). The apostle Paul did not instruct him to pray more earnestly but to "no longer drink only water, but use a little wine." The apostle Paul also left Trophimus, "who was ill, at Miletus" (2 Tim 4:20).

Therefore, as the above examples illustrate, it is vitally important that we *begin* with God's own revelation, and that we begin by working from *all* of his revelation. Often people start with their own practical situation and then slowly work toward God's revelation. But that is the wrong order. If we really want to know the truth about God and his ways, we need to start by listening first to what he himself says. Once we have listened to what he reveals, then we are in the right position to apply that to our daily lives.

WHY WE NEED REVELATION

Now that we have seen the importance of always starting with God's revelation, it is also helpful to say a few words about the necessity of revelation. Revelation is necessary for two reasons: first, the greatness of God and, second, the sinfulness of man.

In the first place, we must not think of God as if he were merely an extraordinarily powerful and intelligent human being. That is a typically pagan idea. In fact, many pagan religions even have carved or cast images of their gods, which look like strong, beautiful, or intelligent human beings or animals. As the apostle Paul says, "Claiming to be wise, they became fools, and exchanged the glory of the immortal God for images resembling mortal man and birds and animals and creeping things" (Rom 1:22–23).

By contrast, God is in a completely different category than we are. He is the Creator, we are creatures. He is divine, we are human. He is infinite, we are finite. He is eternal, we are temporal. As the LORD himself says through the prophet Isaiah, "To whom then will you liken God? . . . It is he who sits above the circle of the earth, and its inhabitants are like grasshoppers" (Isa 40:18, 22). This also means that God's manner of thinking is far beyond what we can fathom with our comparatively miniscule minds. As the prophet Isaiah declares, "Who has measured the Spirit of the Lord, or what man shows him his counsel?" (Isa 40:13) And again, the LORD says, "For as the heavens are higher than the earth, so are my ways higher than your ways and my thoughts than your thoughts" (Isa 55:9).

Since God's thoughts are so high and vast (Ps 139:17), we might be tempted to give up all hope that we could ever understand anything about him. Yet, thankfully, he has revealed himself to us. So our minds do not have to clamber up to him, for he has revealed himself to us in the Bible and, in doing so, he has come near to us (Rom 10:6–8). Furthermore, since God created human beings, he knows our limitations. Thus, when he reveals himself to us, he does it in such a way that we can understand what he is saying. This is also called God's accommodation in revelation. Just as parents communicate to their young children at a level that they can understand, so also God speaks to us in a comprehensible manner.

In the second place, revelation is necessary because we are sinful. Our sinfulness has corrupted our hearts, so that by nature we are inclined to desire and do things that displease God (Col 3:5). However, our sinfulness has also corrupted our minds, so that by nature we do not think about God the way that we should. As the apostle Paul writes, "They are darkened in their understanding, alienated from the life of God because of the ignorance that is in them, due to their hardness of heart" (Eph 4:18). In fact, it is very hard to distinguish between the sinfulness of our desires and the sinfulness of our minds. In the days of Noah the LORD closely connected both of them when he said, "The LORD saw that the wickedness of man was great in the earth, and that every intention of the thoughts of his heart was only evil continually" (Gen 6:5).

If a young child is thinking about his parents in a false and foolish way, then his parents should do something about it. The parents should not think to themselves, "Let's not worry about it. The child will figure it out and correct his own thinking in due time." Of course not! They should teach their children to think correctly about their parents, or about anyone else for that matter. So it is with God, who is our Father in heaven. He reveals the truth and teaches us to think honourably and correctly about him and about ourselves. This does not mean that Christians turn off their brains, but it does mean that our thinking needs to be transformed (Eph 4:23; Col 3:10).

GENERAL AND SPECIAL REVELATION

To this point we have spoken mostly about God's revelation in connection with the Bible. To be sure, that is the primary connection that must be made. However, as the Belgic Confession explains, there are, in fact, two ways in which God reveals himself. It is worthwhile quoting the entire second article.

> We know him by two means: First, by the creation, preservation, and government of the universe; which is before our eyes as a most beautiful book, wherein all creatures, great and small, are as so many letters leading us to perceive clearly the invisible things of God, namely, his eternal power and deity, as the apostle Paul says in Romans 1:20. All these things are sufficient to convict men and leave them without excuse. Second, he makes himself more clearly and fully known to us by his holy and divine Word as far as is necessary for us in this life, to his glory and our salvation.

God's revelation of himself through the "creation, preservation, and government of the universe" is often called general revelation. It is general in the sense that everyone in the world can look at the mountains, the stars, and the animals. It is also general in the sense that when people see how solid the mountains are, how numerous the stars, and how intricate and diverse the animals, they receive some general, but still blurry, perspective on the greatness and wisdom of the Creator.

For example, if someone looks inside a computer, with all of its tiny yet precise components, he might exclaim, "What smart minds must have designed these computer chips!" In a similar way, when someone pauses to admire the complexity of the human brain, or the splendour of a flower, or the force of the ocean waves, he might think to himself, "What a wise God has made all of this! What a powerful God maintains all of this!" This is general revelation. As David once said, "The heavens declare the glory of God, and the sky above proclaims his handiwork" (Ps 19:1–4).

It should not escape our attention that God designed general revelation to reveal something about himself: who he is and how powerful he is. The apostle Paul confirms this in Romans 1:20 when he writes, "For his *invisible attributes*, namely, his eternal power and divine nature, have been clearly perceived, ever since the creation of the world, in the things that have been made." In other words, general revelation is also a very limited revelation. It tells us something about who God is and what he is like, but it does not give us answers to many of the questions that we may have. People ask, "How did this world come into existence? Why is there something rather than nothing? What is the meaning of life? Is there life after death? What is the solution to all the suffering in this world?" Those are all valid questions, but general revelation cannot answer them. To receive the answers to those questions and many more, we must turn to the other book—not the book of creation but the book of Scripture, God's holy Word.

God's special revelation comes to us in the Bible. The opening sentence of the book of Hebrews refers to this. It says that God spoke to his people of old through the prophets, that is, through the Old Testament, but now he has also spoken to us through his Son, that is, through the New Testament. As the Belgic Confession explains, when we compare God's special and general revelation the first thing we notice is how much clearer the special revelation is. It is certainly true, as we read in Psalm 19, that the heavens declare the glory of God (v. 1), but it is also true that "the commandment of the LORD is pure, enlightening the eyes" (v. 8). For example, the tenth commandment is so very plain and straightforward: "You shall not covet." You shall not covet your neighbour's wife, or his house, or anything else that belongs to him. Someone could stare at the stars for a long time, and someone else could carefully study how a human cell functions, but even after years of research they would not know that the LORD is displeased with coveting. Even the apostle Paul says, "For I would not have known what it is to covet if the law had not said, 'You shall not covet'" (Rom 7:7). Yet, in his special revelation God gives one short instruction, the tenth commandment, and the entire matter is crystal clear.

Not only does God's special revelation make things so much more clear, we also learn much more than we ever could from studying creation. It is precisely in God's Word that we learn how the universe was created (Gen 1–2; Heb 11:3), what the meaning of life is (Rom 14:7–8; Phil 1:21–24), what happens when we die (2 Cor 5:1–10), and what the solution is to all the misery in this world (Isa 65:17–25; Col 1:15–20). In fact, it is crucial to affirm that the knowledge of salvation is to be found only in God's special revelation, the Bible. The gospel, which is found throughout the entire Scriptures (see LD 6, Q&A 19), is the "the power of God for salvation to everyone who believes" (Rom 1:16).

In his special revelation God provides us with everything we need to know in order to be saved. That does not mean God tells us everything we might like to know. We may have questions that God does not answer in his Word. Here is one example: if God is almighty, why didn't he prevent Adam and Eve from falling into sin? It is an interesting question, but in the end the only answer we can give is this: God has not revealed the exact reason why he did not prevent the fall into sin. That is also why God's servant Moses reminds us: "The secret things belong to the LORD our God, but the things that are revealed belong to us and to our children forever, that we may do all the words of this law" (Deut 29:29). For our own spiritual well-being it is imperative that we do not speculate beyond what our God has clearly revealed.

It is also important that God's revelation penetrates into the darkest recesses of our heart, rather than merely being a cherished aspect of the spiritual ambiance that surrounds Christians and their activities. What I mean is this: it is one thing to have the Bible in our pews, at our tables, and on our nightstands, but it is another thing to have the truth of God's revelation fundamentally alter the way we think, desire, and act. In short, the Word of God must dwell in us richly (Col 3:16), not just rest on our furniture as an ornament.

A new Christian once commented about the benefits of going to a Bible study group. He observed, "The best evenings are the ones when people's heads are bobbing up and down." That may sound strange, but his further comment clears things up. He added, "If people spend the evening looking at each other and spouting off their opinions, it never goes very deep. But if people are looking down, digging into the Bibles, looking up again to make a comment, and then looking back in the Bible again, the study evening is so much more worthwhile." And that brings us full circle again. How will we ever come to know God rightly if we do not first listen to what God reveals about himself? If listening to her mayor helped Jane understand him better, listening to God's revelation will surely help us understand our Creator properly.

Suggested Readings: Psalm 19:1–6; Romans 1:18–25

QUESTIONS FOR UNDERSTANDING

1. There are people in the world who live by this motto: "My conscience is my guide." Is the conscience a reliable guide? Using a concordance, find some key Scripture passages which speak about the conscience. Summarize what God reveals about the conscience in those passages.
2. What is pragmatic theology? Can you give examples from your life when, perhaps unintentionally, you have tried to fit God's Word into your own desires and your own agenda, rather than allowing God's Word to speak to you first? What are some things that Christians can do to make sure that they do not slip into the approach of pragmatic theology?
3. When we speak of the manner in which God reveals himself to us, what do we mean by accommodation? If God accommodates

himself to our capacities, why are there still parts of the Bible that
are so hard to understand, such as the book of Revelation?

4. List two key difference between general and special revelation, and
discuss the importance of recognizing those differences.

QUESTIONS FOR FURTHER DISCUSSION

1. There are many different religions in the world (e.g., Islam, Taoism,
Buddhism, and Hinduism). Describe the connection between the
great number of religions and the seed of religion. What similarities
or common themes can you discover in all these other religions?
How is Christianity different from all the other religions?

2. Missionaries speak of points of contact. When they bring the
gospel, they look for things in the culture and practices of the
people they are evangelizing that are similar to what the Bible
teaches. Then they try to capitalize on that point of contact so
that people will be drawn to the gospel through something that is
already familiar to them. Could the conscience be a fruitful point
of contact? For example, most people agree that murder is wrong.
Does it help, as a starting point, to say that the Bible also forbids
murder in the sixth commandment? Or does such a point of contact
set our evangelistic effort off on the wrong foot?

3. God gave us his Word through prophets and apostles who lived
a long time ago and who lived in a different country and culture.
Some people therefore say that the Bible is not always relevant to
our modern times and circumstances. How do we respond to those
who think in this way? Hebrews 4:12 may be a helpful starting
point.

4. Scientists spend a lot of time studying creation. Their studies have
led some scientists to conclude that life on this earth has slowly
evolved from one species to another over the course of many
millions of years. The Bible gives a different account of how life
began. In plain language it describes how God created everything
in the span of six days. Is this a conflict between general revelation
and special revelation? If not, how do we explain the difference
between the conclusions of (many) scientists and Scripture?

CHAPTER 3.

HOLY SCRIPTURE

"And we also thank God constantly for this, that when you received the word of God, which you heard from us, you accepted it not as the word of men but as what it really is, the word of God, which is at work in you believers" (1 Thess 2:13). These are remarkable words. On his second missionary journey, the apostle Paul, along with Silas, stopped in the city of Thessalonica. You can read what happened in Acts 17:1–9. Paul and Silas did not stay there very long. In less than one month (Acts 17:2) they left for the neighbouring town of Berea. Yet, when these two men entered the city of Thessalonica, some people who listened to their teaching accepted the words of these men as the very words of God himself.

And they were not mistaken either! The apostle Paul did not rebuke them, saying, "Do not put such high value in our words. After all, we are but mere mortals." On the contrary, Paul and Silas later write to this congregation that they "thank God constantly" because the Thessalonians accepted their word as the word of God. The miraculous process by which God spoke through mere men is called *inspiration*.

Yet how do we know for sure that the Bible was inspired? After all, other religions have their holy books as well. Muslims have the Koran, Hindus have their Vedas, and Sikhs have the Guru Granth Sahib. For those who practise these religions their holy book has some kind of divine authority. So, how can Christians claim that the Bible, both the Old and New

Testaments, are the very word of God? Isn't that at best presumptuous and at worst arrogant? We need to address that question in this chapter.

The doctrine of inspiration has generated other questions as well. People want to know how it happened. Did the Holy Spirit dictate and did such men as Moses and Paul act as secretaries? Or let us use a more modern example. Today we have voice recognition software for our computers. If we speak into the microphone, the words appear on the screen. Is that similar to the way in which God inspired the Scriptures, except that instead of computer software he used such men as Moses and Paul? Or was it quite different from that? Did God merely plant the basic ideas he wanted to convey in the minds of these men? And then did these men work out the rest of the message as they saw best?

These questions are not only interesting but also important. In the end, what is at stake in this discussion about inspiration is the reliability of Holy Scripture. Can we trust what we read in the Bible? Can we trust *everything* that we read in the Bible? The answer to that question is crucial for the strength and stability of our faith.

SCRIPTURE IS GOD-BREATHED

The most well-known text describing the doctrine of inspiration is 2 Timothy 3:16: "All Scripture is breathed out by God and profitable for teaching, for reproof, for correction, and for training in righteousness." In fact, the term *inspiration* is taken from this text. The literal meaning of inspiration is "in-breathing," or as Scripture says in this verse, "breathed by God."

On the sixth day of creation God also breathed for a special purpose. You can read about this in Genesis 2:7, where Moses writes, "Then the LORD God formed the man of dust from the ground and breathed into his nostrils the breath of life, and the man became a living creature." To be sure, the LORD'S in-breathing on the sixth day of creation was different from his in-breathing when he inspired the prophets and apostles. However, it is helpful to compare these two events in order to appreciate their extraordinary nature. It is true that God gives "to all mankind life and breath and everything" (Acts 17:25), but when God first breathed the breath of life into Adam's nostrils, it was a unique event. The Lord simply does not do so with everyone. We do not even read that he did it with Eve. Clearly, divine in-breathing is exceptional. Likewise, when God inspired such men as Moses and Paul to bring his own divine words to his people, he was doing something truly special. He does not fill everyone with his inspired words, but only those special messengers that he chose in his sovereign good-pleasure.

The literal meaning of inspiration, that is, in-breathing, also helps us make the right connection to the Holy Spirit. In the Bible the word for "Spirit" can also mean "breath" or "wind." Thus, the Lord Jesus was using a play on words when he said to Nicodemus, "The wind blows where it wishes, and you hear its sound, but you do not know where it comes from or where it goes. So it is with everyone who is born of the Spirit" (John 3:8). Since there is this tight connection between "Spirit" and "breath," it is not surprising that the Holy Spirit is intimately involved in God's in-breathing of his Scriptures. In fact, the apostle Peter speaks about this when he writes, "For no prophecy was ever produced by the will of man, but men spoke from God as they were carried along by the Holy Spirit" (2 Pet 1:21).

The inspired Scriptures, then, start with God's desire and decision to reveal something to sinful human beings. Moses was not the one who decided one day that he wanted to write a book called Exodus or Deuteronomy. Neither did Moses come up with his own ideas about what should be written in those books. As the apostle Peter says, the origin of prophecy lies with God, not with man (2 Pet 1:21). In this way inspiration is fundamentally different from illumination. The Holy Spirit works in all God's children, shining the light of the knowledge of God into the natural darkness of their hearts and minds (2 Cor 4:6). Indeed, some of God's children are blessed with profound insight into spiritual matters. This can be called illumination, but it is not inspiration. When the Holy Spirit inspired Moses, Paul, or any other Scripture writer, he did not merely illuminate them so that they could share their profound thoughts about God. Instead, the Spirit inspired them so that they spoke the very words of God, words just as divine as if the voice of God himself had breathed them out.

This special work of inspiration applies to the whole Bible. The apostle Paul writes, "*All* Scripture is breathed out by God." There are many different kinds of writing in the Bible. There are historical books (Genesis through Nehemiah), poetic books (Psalms and Proverbs), letters (Romans through 3 John), and apocalyptic books with visions (Daniel, Ezekiel, and Revelation). Some passages in the Bible are easier to understand than others, and some are more difficult. But one thing all chapters and verses of the Bible have in common is this: they are all inspired. Sometimes this is also called *plenary* (i.e., complete) inspiration.

We do not understand exactly how the process of inspiration worked. Without a doubt it was a miracle. However, we can safely say that human authors were much more than dictation machines. One of the gospel writers, Luke, says at the beginning of his account, "It seemed good to me also, having followed all things closely for some time past, to write an orderly account for you, most excellent Theophilus" (Luke 1:3). Obviously Luke was engaged in researching and gathering information about the teachings and sufferings of our Saviour. Yet Luke was not an ordinary biographer. He was not just like so many other biographers who have written books about important people. On the contrary, the Holy Spirit worked in Luke in such a special way that when we read his gospel we can accept it—just as the Thessalonians accepted the words of Paul and Silas—"not as the word of men but as what it really is, the word of God" (1 Thess 2:13).

At the same time, God also did more than merely, in a general sort of way, plant concepts into the minds of those who wrote the Scriptures. Inspiration extends far beyond concepts and reaches right down to the level of words. In fact, at one point in Galatians the apostle Paul builds his argument on just a single letter in the Old Testament, namely, the letter *s*. He writes, "It does not say, 'And to offsprings,' referring to many, but referring to one, 'And to your offspring,' who is Christ" (Gal 3:16).

Clearly, the Holy Spirit was intimately involved in the entire process of writing, from initial idea right through to finished form.

HOW DO WE KNOW FOR SURE?

Now we need to return to the pressing question how we can be confident that the Bible is inspired. Couldn't a Hindu worshipper claim the same for his Vedas? Yes, theoretically, he could, but we are looking for more than a claim; we are looking for well-founded confidence. We need to be able to say, "Yes, we know for certain that the Bible is the inspired Word of God." There are several facts that build that kind of confidence.

- *The Bible presents itself as the inspired word of God.* This can be seen in well-known passages such as Deuteronomy 18:18, 1 Thessalonians 2:13, 2 Timothy 3:16, and 2 Peter 1:21.

- *Jesus believed that the Old Testament was inspired.* For example, in Matthew 19:5 Jesus quotes Genesis 2:24 and introduces it by saying that "he who created [Adam and Eve] . . . said, 'Therefore a man shall leave his father and his mother . . . .'" Now if you look back at Genesis 2:24 you will notice that this is not a direct quote from the mouth of God. God did directly say, "Let us make man in our image" (Gen 1:26), but it was Moses who wrote, "Therefore a man shall leave his father and his mother . . ." (Gen 2:24). Yet, without the slightest hesitation, Jesus attributes those words of Moses to God. Our Saviour believed in inspiration. Peter also believed that Paul's writings were inspired since he puts them on the same level as "the other Scriptures" (2 Pet 3:15–16).

- *The Bible does not hide the ugly or embarrassing facts.* Human beings usually want to make themselves look good. Yet the Holy Spirit prevented the authors of the Bible from skipping over the dark side of our sinful existence. From the adultery of King David (2 Sam 11) to the corruption of Israel (Isa 1) or the denial of Peter (Matt 26:69–75), the miserable reality of sin is duly recorded. This makes the Bible authentic and true to real life.

- *Remarkable prophecies are fulfilled in remarkable ways.* More than seven hundred years before it happened, Isaiah prophesied that a virgin would conceive and give birth to a son (Isa 7:14). About four hundred years before the Ptolemaic (Egyptian) and Seleucid (Syrian) dynasties clashed, Daniel predicted what would happen, even to the point of indicating how Ptolemy VI would be defeated through the bad advice of those who ate at his table (Dan 11:26). Only someone inspired by God could make such detailed and accurate prophecies centuries before the events actually occurred.

- *Humanly speaking, the gospel of salvation is fundamentally counter-intuitive.* That God would send his own well-beloved Son to die a horrific death, all so that ungrateful sinners could be redeemed and enjoy eternal glory as God's own children (Matt 3:17; Rom 5:6–11; 1 John 3:1–3), does not make logical sense. This is not the kind of plan that human beings would devise for salvation. Its complete originality confirms its divine origin (1 Cor 1:18–25).

These five facts set the Bible apart from other holy books, and they might also persuade someone that the Scriptures are inspired. Still, at the end of the day, if someone is truly convinced that the Bible is inspired, it is because the Holy Spirit himself worked that conviction in the person's heart. Confidence that the Bible is God's Word is just as much a miracle as the process of inspiration itself; the Holy Spirit ought to receive the credit for both. The man without the Spirit will not accept Scripture as God's Word, but the man in whom the Spirit works faith will be deeply convinced of this truth (1 Cor 2:11–14). This also means that when someone casts doubt on the inspiration of Scripture, you should not only reason with him cogently, but you should also pray for him fervently. Only the Holy Spirit can penetrate through the hard crust of doubt and plant the tender seed of faith in a human heart. In Article 5 the Belgic Confession sums up this truth nicely when it says:

> We believe without any doubt all things contained in them, not so much because the church receives and approves them as such, but especially because the Holy Spirit witnesses in our hearts that they are from God, and also because they contain the evidence of this in themselves; for even the blind are able to perceive that the things foretold in them are being fulfilled.

SCRIPTURE IS INFALLIBLE

In general, we are taught to read books critically. That does not mean we should read suspiciously. It simply means that we are to read with discernment because we realize that people make mistakes. They make factual errors as well as errors in judgment. When you read books you may therefore come across a statement that is simply not true. Perhaps an author says that the Ming Dynasty ended in 1646; however, when you check the facts you realize that it actually ended in 1644. Also, an author may have all his facts correct, but when you read his conclusions, you may disagree with them. Then you interpret the facts in a rather different way. Normally speaking, this is how we read books.

But when we read the Bible it is different. It is different because its Author is different. The Bible is God-breathed, and God does not lie. He does not make mistakes, and he does not make errors in judgment either. Here are a few passages that confirm this point.

> God is not man, that he should lie, or a son of man, that he should change his mind. Has he said, and will he not do it? Or has he spoken, and will he not fulfill it? (Num 23:19)

> And also the Glory of Israel will not lie or have regret, for he is not a man, that he should have regret (1 Sam 15:29).

> The LORD is righteous in all his ways (Ps 145:17).

As a result the God-breathed Scriptures are as trustworthy and true as God himself. As the psalmist David once declared, "This God—his way is perfect; the word of the LORD proves true; he is a shield for all those who take refuge in him" (Ps 18:30). Notice the progression in this verse. It begins with God himself, affirming that his ways and his actions are perfect. Next it moves to the Word of the LORD. As surely as the LORD's ways are perfect, so certainly his Word is flawless.

This trustworthiness of Scripture gives us a place of security and refuge. This world is full of people who twist and warp the truth (Ps 116:11). It can be very discouraging when people, even people whom you love, do not always deal with you honestly and sincerely. However, even if the world is filled with an ocean of deception, there is one island of flawless and reliable truth: the Word of God! We call this the *infallibility*, or *inerrancy*, of Holy Scripture.

Of course, there are people who question the infallibility of Scripture. They say that there are contradictions in the Bible. For example, in John 1:18 we read, "No has ever seen God." Yet in Exodus 24:10 we are told that Moses and Aaron, Nadab and Abihu, as well as seventy elders "saw the God of Israel." Is this a contradiction in the Bible? No, not if we take a moment to consider how language is being used in each verse.

Let us take an example from daily life. Someone may ask, "Have you ever seen the back of your head?" Upon hearing that question some people might be inclined to answer, "No." Since your eyes are firmly fixed in the front of your head, you cannot see the back of your head. Others would be inclined to say, "Yes." If you have two mirrors, you can arrange them in such a way that you see the back of your head. However, another person may reply and say, "Yes, but technically speaking, you do not actually see the back of your head; you see a *reflection* of the back of your head in the mirror." That is true, but it is also true that it is perfectly legitimate to say, "Yes, I've seen the back of my head in the mirror." That is not a lie. That is simply the way language works.

Let us return now to John 1:18 and Exodus 24:10. In the first place, since God is invisible (1 Tim 1:17), it is impossible to see him in his natural, divine essence. That is what John 1:18 means. However, on various occasions, for a short time, God has taken on a visible form. For example, he appeared to Abraham in the form of a man (Gen 18:1–2). Daniel also had a vision in which he saw God in the form of a man with white clothing and white hair (Dan 7:9). In a similar way, on Mount Sinai, the leaders and elders of Israel saw a special, visible manifestation of God. But they did not see the invisible essence of God. Thus there is no contradiction between John 1:18 and Exodus 24:10. This also applies to other so-called contradictions in the Bible. If we look at the passages in their context and understand well how the language is being used, the so-called contradictions turn out to be no contradictions at all.

SCRIPTURE HAS PERFECTIONS

In addition to being flawless, Scripture also has certain special attributes that are often called the *perfections* of Scripture. We will look briefly at the four most common ones: authority, necessity, clarity, and sufficiency.

In the first place, God's Word is the first and final *authority* in all matters related to our Christian faith. This can be best understood if we compare it to the infallibility of Scripture. As mentioned earlier, just as God does not lie, so also his Word is flawless. Similarly, just as God is sovereign over everything (2 Chron 20:6), so also his Word comes to us with weight and authority. In Article 6, the Belgic Confession summarizes it in this way: "We receive all these books, and these only, as holy and canonical, for the regulation, foundation, and confirmation of our faith." When it says "all these books," the Belgic Confession is referring to the list of sixty-six books in Article 5. These sixty-six books are called the *canon* of Scripture. Canon means the *rule*, or the *standard*. So, in practical terms, in all matters of faith, when we want to know the truth, we turn to the standard of the Bible, in which God has the final say about everything he reveals.

Secondly, God's Word is *necessary*. We touched on this already in chapter 2. Since God is so lofty and so holy, we need him to teach us about himself and the salvation that he has worked for us in Jesus Christ. These are things that we, as finite creatures, cannot figure out on our own. Moreover, this is even truer now that we live after the fall into sin. Sin has clouded and corrupted our minds. We can still think, of course, but by nature we will not think *correctly* about God. For this reason having God's Word is not a pleasant luxury but a real necessity.

Thirdly, God's Word has its own *clarity*. This does not mean that everything in the Bible is instantly easy to understand. Even the apostle Peter says that there are challenging passages in the letters of the apostle Paul:

"There are some things in them that are hard to understand, which the ignorant and unstable twist to their own destruction, as they do the other Scriptures" (2 Pet 3:16). But this should not discourage us. We have received a great blessing. The Lord Jesus Christ has sent the Holy Spirit to dwell in us and remain with us forever (John 14:16–17). This Holy Spirit is the very same one who inspired the Scriptures in the first place. Certainly, the Author of Scripture will be able to help us, the readers, understand his own Word. If there is a lack of clarity or confusion, then the problem is with our understanding, not with God's revelation. However, prayerfully and patiently we will grow in understanding what the Lord teaches us in the gospel.

Finally, what God has revealed in Scripture is *sufficient* for salvation and for worshipping the Lord in a manner that is pleasing to him. It is true: the Bible does not give us an answer to every possible question that might arise in our minds. There are certain things that the LORD in his divine wisdom has decided to keep to himself (Deut 29:29). But what he has revealed is enough. The Belgic Confession sums it up in this way in Article 7:

> We believe that this Holy Scripture fully contains the will of God and that all that man must believe in order to be saved is sufficiently taught therein. The whole manner of worship which God requires of us is written in it at length. It is therefore unlawful for any one, even for an apostle, to teach otherwise than we are now taught in Holy Scripture: yes, even if it be an angel from heaven, as the apostle Paul says (Gal 1:8). Since it is forbidden to add to or take away anything from the Word of God (Deut 12:32), it is evident that the doctrine thereof is most perfect and complete in all respects.

The words of men—no matter how intelligent or wise they may be—can never equal the Word of God. The difference is simply too great. It is the difference between Creator and creature. Therefore we need to be content and trust that whatever we really need to know about salvation and worship, the Lord has taught us. It is sufficient.

NO MORE INSPIRED REVELATIONS TODAY

The sufficiency of Scripture also warns us to be careful with people who claim to have direct, personal revelations from God and who treat those private revelations as if they were inspired. Let us remember that the inspiration, or in-breathing, of Scripture was a very special, unique event. It was not a common everyday experience.

In addition, the Lord inspired the prophets and apostles for the special purpose of laying the foundation of truth upon which he will be building his church until he returns on the clouds of heaven. The apostle Paul speaks of this in Ephesians 2:19–22:

> So then you are no longer strangers and aliens, but you are fellow citizens with the saints and members of the household of God, built on the foundation of the apostles and prophets, Christ Jesus himself being the cornerstone, in whom the whole structure, being joined together, grows into a holy temple in the Lord. In him you also are being built together into a dwelling place for God by the Spirit.

Once the foundation of a building is laid, that task is finished. It does not need to be repeated. The Lord used inspiration for foundation work. However, now our Lord is beyond the foundation stage in building his church. Now Jesus Christ, through the Holy Spirit, who uses the inspired Word, is busy building the walls of his church and making us living stones within those walls (1 Pet 2:4–5). The era of inspiration ended with the apostles; however, the time for preaching and studying the inspired Word is most certainly still with us (2 Tim 4:2).

Suggested Readings: 2 Timothy 3:10–17; 2 Peter 1:16–21

QUESTIONS FOR UNDERSTANDING

1. What is the difference between illumination and inspiration? Define both terms as carefully as you can.
2. Read the Belgic Confession, Articles 3–7. In your own words, summarize the main points of Articles 3, 5, and 7.

3. Identify the four attributes, or perfections, of Scripture and briefly describe each one.

4. What is the canon of Scripture? What are the apocryphal books? Can we use them? See the Belgic Confession, Article 6.

QUESTIONS FOR FURTHER DISCUSSION

1. In your experience, what kind of doubts do people have concerning the trustworthiness of the Bible? If possible, give three concrete examples and explain how you would respond to each one.

2. When a fellow Christian is having difficulty understanding a certain passage in the Bible, what should he do, and what can you do to help him? Try to list four different things and explain why each one is important.

3. Use an online search engine to learn about the doctrine of abrogation in Islam. How does this doctrine compare with the way that Scripture speaks about itself, for example, in Matthew 5:17–18 and Revelation 22:18–19?

4. Sometimes people claim to have a direct message from God and will make bold predictions or strong demands. Read Deuteronomy 18:14–22 (esp. vv. 21–22) and 1 John 4:1–3. Referring to these passages, explain how we should deal with such people.

CHAPTER 4.

KNOWING AND TRUSTING GOD

In the Garden of Gethsemane, Jesus Christ prayed to his Father, "And this is eternal life, that they know you the only true God, and Jesus Christ whom you have sent" (John 17:3). This makes it clear that knowing God is very important. In fact, it is eternally important.

However, there are different ways in which we may know someone. For example, let us suppose that there are two students at university, the first is named Jane, the other Danielle. Jane asks Danielle, "Do you know Susan?" And Danielle replies, "Yes, I know Susan. She is the chemistry major who just won the annual science award." "That's right!" says Jane. So, it is true: Danielle knows Susan. But *how well* does she know Susan? Perhaps she has only heard Susan's name and seen her picture in the student newspaper. Maybe she has seen Susan walking on campus or taken a science class with her. But this does not mean that Danielle and Susan are close friends. In sum, Danielle's knowledge of Susan may be very limited.

Now let us consider another example. Suppose an extended family is going to have a reunion. Many of the relatives have not seen each other for a long time. The organizers of the reunion would like to have some live background music. One day Jack is talking to his cousin Brent and says, "Your father plays the piano quite well. Why don't you ask him if he would play at the reunion?" However, Brent replies, "That will never happen. I *know* my father. Yes, he's very musical, but he becomes so dreadfully nervous when he has to play in front of a crowd. No, I can already give you the answer now. He will not agree to play piano at the reunion." Obviously this is a situation completely different from the first one. Both Danielle and Brent use the same word: to know. But when Brent says, "I *know* my father," he is emphasizing the depth of his knowledge. Indeed, he knows his father so well that he can even anticipate accurately how his father would respond if he were asked to play the piano at the reunion. Without a doubt there is a special way in which parents and children know each other.

So, how are we to know God? Is it sufficient to know about God in the way Danielle, in the first example above, knows something about Susan? Many people know about God that way. As we learned in chapter 2, people can obtain a notion that God exists from general revelation. They can also have some sense of his power and wisdom. However, they do not really know him as children know their father. That kind of knowledge comes only from special revelation, that is, from the inspired Scriptures, as we learned in chapters 2 and 3. Moreover, it is this kind of familiar and familial knowledge that Jesus Christ was praying about in John 17. At the end of his prayer he says to his Father, "O righteous Father, even though the world does not know you, I know you" (John 17:25). So, Christ knows him as the Son knows his very own, eternal Father. At the same time, Christ does not keep this knowledge to himself, for he continues, "I made known to them your name, and I will continue to make it known . . ." (John 17:26; also see John 1:18). As we learn from Christ, we come to know God, not as Danielle knows Susan, but as earthly children know their heavenly Father.

KNOWING OUR LIMITS IN KNOWING OUR GOD

To this point we have compared our knowledge of God to the kind of knowledge that children have of their parents. It is a close, deep, and far-reaching knowledge. But how far can we take this comparison? It is true that a human child can know his human father well, even very well. But it is a different thing for a *human* being to know a *divine* being. After all, God is the Creator, and we are just creatures. He is eternal, and we are temporal. He is infinite, and we are finite. In addition, there are passages in the Bible which clearly state that human beings cannot completely understand God. Here are a few examples:

> Great is the LORD, and greatly to be praised, and his greatness is unsearchable (Ps 145:3).

> Who has measured the Spirit of the LORD, or what man shows him his counsel? . . . The LORD is the everlasting God, the Creator of the ends of the earth. He does not faint or grow weary; his understanding is unsearchable (Isa 40:13, 28).

> Oh, the depth of the riches and wisdom and knowledge of God! How unsearchable are his judgments and how inscrutable his ways! (Rom 11:33)

In these passages the LORD is not speaking about people who only know him from general revelation. On the contrary, he is speaking to his own people, who have learned about him from the inspired prophets and apostles. Even believers cannot fathom God. That is to say, they may know him well, but they do not know him *fully*. There is a boundary, a border line, to their knowledge of God. Once their minds reach that boundary line, there is a big sign posted that says, "No trespassing by human beings" (see also Deut 29:29).

These truths are summarized in Article 1 of the Belgic Confession. There we confess that God is "eternal, *incomprehensible*, invisible, immutable, infinite . . . ." The first and last word in that list are connected to the second one. Unlike us, God is both eternal and infinite. Therefore we cannot fully comprehend him, his ways, or his decisions. His ways and his thoughts are simply too grand and glorious; our tiny little minds cannot figure them out (Isa 55:8–9).

There are at least two areas of doctrine in which it is critical that we recognize the limits of our understanding. They are God's providence and his electing grace in Jesus Christ. We will deal with both of these doctrines later on in this book (chapters 8 and 12). However, it is good for us to touch on them briefly here, in connection with the limits of our knowledge. Concerning providence the Belgic Confession says in Article 13:

And as to His actions surpassing human understanding, we will not curiously inquire farther than our capacity allows us. But with the greatest humility and reverence we adore the just judgments of God, which are hidden from us, and we content ourselves that we are pupils of Christ, who have only to learn those things which he teaches us in his Word, without transgressing these limits.

Concerning God's providence many questions can enter our minds. Why does God allow earthquakes to cause so much destruction? Why does God send me sickness, whereas unbelievers keep on living in very good health? Why does God give some people wealth while others remain poor? We are curious people; we have many questions. Sometimes our questions are fully answered in the Bible. Other times our questions are only partially answered in the Bible. There are also times when the Lord does not give us any answer in the Bible. Our question simply remains a question. But the key thing is this: in discussing all our questions we may go as far as the Bible goes—but not a centimetre farther. That is what the Belgic Confession means when it says we have "only to learn those things which he teaches us in his Word, *without transgressing these limits*."

In a similar way the Canons of Dort remind us how the doctrine of God's eternal election should be taught. We confess that this doctrine is revealed in both the Old and the New Testament; however, then the Canons continue by saying:

Therefore, also today this doctrine should be taught in the church of God, for which it was particularly intended, in its proper time and place, provided it be done with a spirit of discretion, in a reverent and holy manner, without inquisitively prying into the ways of the Most High, to the glory of God's most holy name, and for the living comfort of His people (1.14).

Also concerning the doctrine of election God's children have many questions. Why does God pick one person for salvation and not another? Why didn't God just choose to save everyone? How can a loving God pass over certain people and allow them to be punished eternally? Now, the Bible does speak about election; therefore, we also ought to speak about it and teach it. But we must be careful to stick to our limits. We must not try to pry and peek into things that God has not revealed to us.

There are theologians who try to go beyond Scripture and come up with their own answers on the basis of their own human reasoning. This is sometimes called *speculative theology*. Theologians are not the only ones who sometimes push beyond the limits. Well-intentioned adults and genuinely curious children do so as well. But in all these cases speculation needs to be replaced with discretion and humility. As the apostle Paul reminds us in Romans 9:19–21, we have to remember that God is the Potter and we are the clay. As "jars of clay" (2 Cor 4:7) we should be joyfully content to pass on what our Saviour Jesus has taught us in his Word. We should also be vigilant that we do not go beyond that.

Perhaps it helps to think of it in this way: Parents do not share everything they know with their children. This may well be for the children's own benefit. For example, does a four-year-old need to know everything about the household budget? Isn't it better for a young child to live life without fretting about family finances? Furthermore, if we can all agree on that, we should be able to extend the analogy and grant that it is a good thing God does not reveal more than he does. Or are we forgetting our status as *children* of God?

ATHEISM, AGNOSTICISM, AND RATIONALISM

Some people insist that there simply is no God. They are called *atheists*. Bertrand Russell, Christopher Hitchens, and Richard Dawkins are names of well-known atheists of the twentieth and twenty-first centuries. Atheists believe that there is no God. Of course, they cannot prove this. Even Bertrand Russell (1872–1970), who was a highly acclaimed philosopher, wrote, "I do not think that there is a conclusive argument by which one can prove that there is not a God."[1] At least on this point, Russell is entirely correct. However, logically speaking, this also means that since atheism is neither proven nor provable, it must be a belief. In fact, even

1. Bertrand Russell, *Last Philosophical Testament 1943–68*, ed. John G. Slater (London: Routledge, 1997), 91.

though atheists may disagree, they are following a false *religion* that denies the existence of God.

Truth be told, it is very hard to be a consistent atheist. Someone once said to me, "I'm an atheist, so long as I don't go hiking in the forest." If anyone walks in the beauty of creation, and actually stops to think about what he sees, he will be hard-pressed to believe that there is no divine Designer of all the intricate splendour that fills every corner of creation. Yet there are those who strenuously suppress this glaringly obvious truth and maintain that there is no God. The Lord himself gives a clear evaluation of this atheism. He calls it foolish. "The fool says in his heart, 'There is no God'" (Ps 14:1). Furthermore, the folly of atheism will be fully revealed on the final day, when every knee will bow before Jesus, and every tongue will confess that God exists and that Christ is the Lord (Phil 2:10–11).

Other people are uncertain about whether God exists. They do not want to say, "God exists." Neither do they want to say, "God does *not* exist." Instead, they try to find some middle ground on which they can stand by saying, "We simply don't know. For us the existence of God is an open question without a definite answer." These people are called *agnostics*, which literally means *those who do not know*.

Agnostics will often say that they are simply being honest with themselves. On the one hand, they might give some credit to the argument that since creation is so well designed, it must have a divine Designer. On the other hand, they are also persuaded by the argument that if God exists, it is shocking, or perhaps even objectionable, that he allows so much evil and suffering to occur in the world. In the minds of the agnostics these arguments, both for and against God's existence, therefore cancel each other out, leaving them in a state of uncertainty.

In reality, though, agnosticism often works out to be essentially the same thing as atheism. Agnostics may say that they are not sure whether God exists, but most of them go ahead and live their daily lives as if they were, in fact, certain that God does not exist. They do not take time to learn more about God in order to see if greater certainty might be gained. They do not take time to worship God and explore the possibility that he might be more real than they ever anticipated. Instead, most agnostics find an intellectual escape route by saying, "I don't know if God exists, and I'm content to leave it at that." Practically speaking, they carry on living as if they are completely unaccountable to God. In this regard agnosticism is as foolish as atheism.

Not only are agnosticism and atheism similar in practice, they are also rooted in the same error. That error is rationalism. *Rationalism* is the conviction that human reason is the sufficient, supreme, and final judge in all things. Simply put, rationalism says, "If it makes sense to my mind, I will accept it. Otherwise, I reject it." There is an enormous problem with rationalism, and that is pride. Even Job, who was an upright man (Job 1:1), fell into this temptation. He had suffered greatly, losing all his wealth and his children in a single day (Job 1). Shortly thereafter he lost his health as well (Job 2). As he discusses these afflictions with his friends, it becomes clear that Job wants a reasonable and rational explanation. He wonders, "Why should I suffer so much even though I have been faithful to the LORD and his commands?" And he wants the LORD himself to provide the answer (Job 31:35).

Eventually the LORD does answer him, but the response is different from what Job initially expected. The LORD does not explain why Job had to suffer. Instead, he asks Job a series of questions such as: "Where were you when I laid the foundation of the earth?" (38:4), "Have you commanded the morning since your days began, and caused the dawn to know its place?" (38:12), and "Can you lift up your voice to the clouds, that a flood of waters may cover you?" (38:34) For four chapters in a row (Job 38–41) the LORD asks Job question after question. At the end and in reply Job says, "I have uttered what I did not understand, things too wonderful for me, which I did not know" (42:3). In other words, Job was humbled; his pride was subdued. He admits that his small human mind is not the supreme or final judge. Rather, he learns to trust that what God says and plans is the final authority. This is true for all of us. Rationalism needs to be replaced by repentance and humility.

WHAT IS FAITH?

Faith is not anti-intellectual. Faith is not opposed to reason. However, faith is convinced of things that go beyond our intellectual capacity. The most well-known definition of faith comes from Hebrews 11:1. There we read, "Now faith is the assurance of things hoped for, the conviction of things not seen." There is a saying, "I'll believe it when I see it." People like visible and tangible proof. Someone may say to you, "I'll give you $10,000." After hearing that, you might well think to yourself, "That is wonderful, but I'll believe it when I actually see you put that money in my hand!"

Too many people treat God as if he were just another human being. They refuse to trust God completely until he actually does what they want him to do. If they are sick, they might agree to believe in God . . . so long as he heals them. If they are poor, they may agree to trust God . . . as soon as he gives them some more material wealth. But this approach does not show true faith, for it consistently begins at the wrong point. It starts with the idea that the holy God, like sinful human beings, is not always trustworthy. However, we must not think of God as if he were a supreme human being. *All* of his promises come true; *all* of his words are fulfilled (Luke 21:33). Our starting point must be that God is always completely trustworthy.

It is for this reason that the Apostles' Creed is careful to say, "I believe in God the Father . . . I believe in Jesus Christ, his only-begotten Son . . . [and] I believe in the Holy Spirit." That is to say, in the first place, faith is trusting in Someone, Someone who is entirely unique and eternally faithful. That special someone is our triune God. At the last supper that he had with his disciples, the Lord Jesus Christ spoke of faith in this way: "Let not your hearts be troubled. Believe in God; believe also in me" (John 14:1). So, a one-word definition for faith is *trust*.

The Heidelberg Catechism captures this same emphasis. Consider, for example, Lord's Day 7, Q&A 21:

What is true faith? True faith is a sure knowledge whereby I accept as true all that *God* has revealed to us in his Word. At the same time, it is a firm confidence that not only to others, but also to me, *God* has granted forgiveness of sins, everlasting righteousness, and salvation, out of mere grace, only for the sake of Christ's merits. This faith the Holy Spirit works in my heart by the gospel.

Please notice that the Catechism describes faith as a *sure knowledge* and a *firm confidence*. However, both the knowledge and the confidence are directed toward and founded upon God—the God who never lies and always keeps his word (Num 23:19). In fact, the apostle Paul adds, "As surely as God is faithful, our word to you has not been Yes and No . . . . For all the promises of God find their Yes in him. That is why it is through him that we utter our Amen to God for his glory" (2 Cor 1:18, 20).

Many things about the Christian faith cannot be fully and rationally explained. How could the eternal Son of God be born as a baby in a manger? How could Jesus Christ rise from the dead? How can God be so compassionate as to forgive all of my many, many sins? Our brains cannot figure out all these things. But the Holy Spirit, who is God, works faith in our hearts through the inspired gospel, so that we trust that what God says is true, and it is true for me, too! *That* is what true faith is.

DEFENDING THE FAITH

Apologetics is the study of how to make a reasonable defence of the Christian faith, especially when there are opponents who undermine or even ridicule the truths of Scripture. Christians should be willing and able to defend their faith. The apostle Peter instructs us with these words: "But in your hearts honour Christ the Lord as holy, always being prepared to make a defense to anyone who asks you for a reason for the hope that is in you; yet do it with gentleness and respect" (1 Pet 3:15; see also 2 Cor 10:5). Furthermore, Acts 17 is a classic example of how the apostle Paul went into the pagan city of Athens and clearly defended the identity of the true and living God (Acts 17:22–31).

It is also instructive to read how the people responded to Paul's speech. God's Word says, "Now when they heard of the resurrection of the dead, some mocked. But others said, 'We will hear you again about this'" (Acts 17:32). Both groups heard exactly the same message, but they reacted in two very different ways. This reminds us to be sober and realistic in our apologetics. We may give a very clear, concise, and courageous defence of the Christian faith, but we cannot generate faith in someone's heart by argumentation. As Acts 17 reminds us, and as Lord's Day 7 summarizes for us, faith is a miracle that is worked in someone's heart by the power of the Holy Spirit, not by the power of persuasive arguments (1 Cor 2:4).

As believers we may be disappointed that atheists, agnostics, and other unbelievers are so persistent in their rejection of God. But we should not be entirely surprised by this. As the apostle Paul explains, "The natural person does not accept the things of the Spirit of God, for they are folly to him, and he is not able to understand them because they are spiritually discerned" (1 Cor 2:14). Also, as much as we may long and pray for the conversion of those with whom we speak, we must remember our primary motivation for defending the faith ought to be promoting the honour of God. In destroying "every lofty opinion raised against the knowledge of God" (2 Cor 10:5) our first goal is to uphold the good and glorious reputation of our Redeemer.

Suggested Reading: Isaiah 55:6–11

QUESTIONS FOR UNDERSTANDING

1. Define atheism and agnosticism. Explain how each is related to rationalism.
2. What is speculative theology? Give examples of common questions that adults have which run the risk of treading into the territory of speculative theology. Provide some more examples of how children's questions can step over the boundary of what is revealed. How do we draw the fine line between acknowledging that the answer we want is not revealed and realizing that perhaps we have

not searched hard enough in the Bible to find it? In other words, are we sometimes too quick to say, "The Bible doesn't talk about that"?

3. Read James 2:14–26. What is the key difference between living faith and dead faith? Sometimes the fruit of faith is quite small. What should we do if the spiritual harvest in our own life is quite meagre? How do we avoid slipping into a spiral of doubt about our own salvation? Make use of Canons of Dort 1.16 in your answer.

4. Faith is trust. Expand on this statement with a few descriptive phrases that elaborate on what kind of trust faith should be. One example might be as follows: faith is trust *that never gives up hoping in God, no matter how gloomy the future may look.* Can you think of more?

QUESTIONS FOR FURTHER DISCUSSION

1. Read Genesis 3:1–7 about the fall into sin. Would it be accurate to say that Eve sinned by desiring to transgress the limits of her human knowledge and obtain divine knowledge? Why is it that we sometimes have such a hard time being content to learn what God teaches us in his Word? Why are we often eager to know the very things he has decided not to reveal? How can we keep our curiosity in check?

2. Have you had any experience in speaking to agnostics? If so, explain how you spoke to them. Was it effective? What might you improve on next time? Run through these same questions again, only this time applying them to atheists.

3. When we are defending the Christian faith we sometimes use certain arguments to persuade people that their ideas about God are false. At the same time we know that faith does not rest on logical arguments but upon God's inspired Word (LD 7, Q&A 21). How can we on the one hand use reason in our apologetics, but on the other hand prevent reason from becoming the foundation of our faith?

4. As children of God we are to know him and trust him as children know and trust their own earthly fathers. Yet what about those situations in which earthly fathers have been mostly, or entirely,

absent from their children's life, or in which they have been present but then in an abusive manner? How can such children learn to know and trust their heavenly Father? How can we help people like that, also later in life, overcome the psychological and emotional hurdles that they understandably face?

CHAPTER 5.

GOD'S NAMES AND PERFECTIONS

Consider the following scenario. A father is looking for a violin teacher for his daughter. One potential teacher asks the father to describe his daughter. He says, "Well, she is eleven years old. She is very eager to learn how to play the violin. She can be quite shy at times, but once you come to know her, I'm sure you'll find that she's friendly and talkative." Of course, a father naturally speaks about the good qualities of his child. However, to begin this lesson we want to focus on something else, namely, the difference between *essence* and *attributes*. We do not use these words every day. Since people do sometimes use them to describe God, let us explore these terms a little further.

In the example above, the father listed three attributes of his daughter. First, she is eleven years old. Second, she is eager to learn. Third, she can be shy. Now let us fast-forward three years into the future. The daughter is no longer eleven years old; now she is fourteen. She is no longer eager to learn how to play the violin; in fact, she stopped taking lessons after only one year. Moreover, by now she has lost almost all of her shyness; she loves talking to almost anyone who is willing to listen to her. In other words, in the span of a few years these three attributes of the daughter have all changed, noticeably if not dramatically.

Even though his daughter has changed in many ways, without hesitation the father will still say, "She is my daughter!" Being a daughter is simply an unchangeable part of who she is. It is part of her essence.

Attributes can change, but essence remains the same. In particular the ancient Greek philosopher Aristotle made extensive use of this distinction between essence and attributes.

Many theologians have taken over this distinction, and they use the terms *essence* and *attributes* to describe God. God's essence is his divine nature or divine being. Turning to his attributes, we could mention that God is eternal, infinite, almighty, wise, holy, just, and good. But as soon as we say this, we run directly into an obvious problem. According to Aristotle's philosophy, attributes can change but essence remains the same. Is that also true of God? Could God change his attribute of holiness into something else and still remain God? Could God switch from being infinite to finite, all the while leaving his divine essence intact? The answer is no. In short, the concepts of essence and attributes do not work with God as they work with human beings. When Scripture says, "God is love" (1 John 4:16), then we should understand that love is part of the very essence of God. God cannot alter or abandon his love and still remain God. That is impossible. Love is simply and eternally part of who he is.

For this reason we also speak sometimes of the *names* and *perfections* of God, rather than of his essence and attributes. That is the approach we will take in this chapter.

THE NAMES OF GOD

Today when parents give their child a name, there are a few motivations that often play a role. Sometimes a particular name is chosen because it is part of a family tradition. For example, a son may be named after his father or grandfather. Other times parents chose a name because they like the way it sounds. Still other parents consider the meaning of the name, and they want their child to grow up to be the kind of person whose character matches that meaning.

In the Bible, when God gives someone a name he focuses on the meaning. For example, God changed the name of Abram to Abraham, and then he immediately added, "I have made you the father of a multitude of nations" (Gen 17:5). That is exactly what Abraham means: father of many nations. So, let us apply this to God's own name, I AM WHO I AM. This same name is also indicated by the word *Yahweh*. In many Bible translations, it is written as *LORD*, with all capital letters. This name should not be confused with *Lord*, which means ruler or master. We will return to the title *Lord* a little later.

I AM WHO I AM or Yahweh

God revealed his name, I AM WHO I AM, to Moses at the burning bush at Mount Horeb. God appears there to Moses because his people in Egypt are suffering in their slavery (Exod 2:23). God hears their groans, and he is going to do something about it. That is why he comes to Horeb: to send Moses to free his people from their cruel bondage in Egypt (Exod 3:9–10). Moses feels inadequate for such a large task, but God still sends him and promises to be with him (Exod 3:12). It is at this point that Moses asks about God's name. He says, "If I come to the people of Israel and say to them, 'The God of your fathers has sent me to you,' and they ask me, 'What is his name?' what shall I say to them?" (Exod 3:13). Then God answers, "I AM WHO I AM . . . Say this to the people of Israel, 'I AM has sent me to you'" (Exod 3:14).

There are a few important things to notice about the revelation of this divine name. In the first place, I AM WHO I AM is sympathetic toward the sufferings of his people. There are those who think that, for the most part, God is uninterested and uninvolved in what happens here on earth. These people are called deists. However, as the Holy Spirit makes clear in Exodus 3, I AM WHO I AM is not the God of the deists. On the contrary, he listens, he has compassion, and he acts to save his people. In short, I AM is the God of redeeming action.

Second, I AM WHO I AM is consistent. Yes, he is taking action to save his people, but this is also exactly what he promised to do many years earlier (Exod 3:17; see also Gen 15:12–16). When it concerns fellow human beings, sometimes we never quite know where we stand. They make promises. But will they keep them? They put on a brave face. But are they really terrified inside? With people we often ask, "Is this person truly all that he says he is?" However, by revealing his name our God answers that question even before we ask it. He says, "I AM WHO I AM." That is, I AM consistently WHO I AM.

Third, I AM WHO I AM remains faithful through the generations of his covenant. (We will study the doctrine of the covenant in more detail in chapter 11.) Immediately after God reveals his name, he adds, "Say this to the people of Israel, 'The LORD, the God of your fathers, the God of Abraham, the God of Isaac, and the God of Jacob, has sent me to you.' This is my name forever, and thus I am to be remembered throughout all generations" (Exod 3:15). In other words, God does not change who he is, or how he acts, from day to day. In fact, he does not change from generation to generation either. Jacob could rely on the fact that God would treat him in the same way that he treated his father Isaac and his grandfather Abraham.

Fourth, I AM WHO I AM cannot be defined by comparing him to anyone or anything else. As the LORD says through the prophet Isaiah, "To whom then will you compare me, that I should be like him?" (Isa 40:25). In other words, the only one who can be properly compared to God is God himself. That is why his name sounds redundant: *I AM* WHO *I AM*. However, in this case the repetition is full of meaning and purpose. God is saying that he, and he alone, is God. You cannot equate him with idols, or angels, or human beings, or anything or anyone else.

Therefore, in sum, God is the entirely unique, always consistent, redemptively active God who remains faithful from generation to generation in the line of his covenant people. All of that is compressed into his most special name: I AM WHO I AM or *Yahweh*. It is also helpful to know that a shortened form of this name is *Jah*; it can be found in names such as Elijah and Adonijah as well as in the common exclamation of praise: Hallelujah.

Yahweh Sebaoth

About two hundred and fifty times you will read in Scripture one of his combined names, the LORD of hosts, *Yahweh Sebaoth* (1 Sam 1:3; 1 Sam 15:2; Isa 5:7; Hag 1:2, 5, 7, etc.) This compound name emphasizes that this redemptively active God controls all the angels and all the nations and creatures of the earth, including the heavenly bodies such as the sun, moon, and stars. In short, God is the Supreme Commander who can issue an order to any creature, either visible or invisible, and that creature simply must obey. This is the meaning of *Yahweh Sebaoth*.

God Almighty or *El Shaddai*

The LORD used this name when he appeared to Abram and confirmed his covenant with him. He said, "I am God Almighty; walk before me, and be blameless" (Gen 17:1; see also Exod 6:3). There is some discussion about the exact meaning of the second part of this name: *Shaddai*. No definite conclusion has been reached, but from the way this name is used in the Bible it is clear that it highlights just how high and exalted our God is. There is no one more powerful than he is, no one more gracious, no one wiser. In every possible way God is surpassingly great. This is the meaning captured in his name *God Almighty*.

Lord or Adonai

On other occasions Scripture ascribes certain titles to God. The most frequent one is *Lord* (spelled without all capitals), which is literally *Adonai*. This title describes God's exalted position as the ruler over all. In 1 Timothy 6:15 the apostle Paul uses an expanded version of this title when he describes God as "the blessed and only Sovereign, the King of kings and Lord of lords." This title also reminds us of our position. Since God is our Lord, we are his servants (LD 13, Q&A 34). Servants have a clear purpose in life: they are to obey their master's commands, promptly and wholeheartedly (Luke 17:10).

Other descriptions of God

There are many other vivid descriptions of God in the Bible. He is called the "horn of my salvation" (Ps 18:2), "my shepherd" (Ps 23:1), "the Holy One" (2 Kings 19:22), and "the Ancient of Days" (Dan 7:9)—to list but a few. Each one of these descriptive titles emphasizes a certain aspect of God's character or his activity. At the same time, we must remember that since God is God *Most High* (Ps 78:35), he far transcends these descriptions. That is to say, God is our shepherd, but he is also much more than our shepherd. He is our Father, our Redeemer, our Guide, and our King, too. We should be careful that we do not cling to one particular description of God (e.g., Redeemer) to the detriment of other descriptions (e.g., King). True faith involves accepting *all* that God reveals about himself, not just our favourite parts (LD 7, Q&A 21).

THE PERFECTIONS OF GOD

The Belgic Confession describes God as the one who is "a simple and spiritual being; he is eternal, incomprehensible, invisible, immutable, infinite, almighty, perfectly wise, just, good, and the overflowing fountain of all good" (Art 1). As mentioned above, according to many theologians the Confession refers here to the attributes of God. However, they might better be called the *perfections* of God. Even though the Belgic Confession only adds the word "perfectly" to "wise," it could just as well have added it to the other terms it mentions. God is also perfectly immutable and perfectly just. Let us take a brief look at each perfection in this list plus two more: God's grace and his holiness.

Simple

Is God simple? There are some things about God that are very difficult to understand. So it sounds strange to describe God as simple. However, here *simple* does not have its more common meaning. It indicates that God is not compound; that is to say, he is not a collection of various, different parts. By contrast, our bodies are compound. We are made up of a head, chest, arms, legs, etc. But God is non-compound, or, to say it more positively, he is simple. This may all sound rather abstract, but it is important when we speak about the perfections of God. When human beings administer justice, they sometimes compromise or even cancel out their compassion. God is not like that. He is perfectly and simultaneously just and merciful. He is perfectly and simultaneously almighty and good. None of his perfections ever compromise or cancel out any other perfection. In this way God is simple, and his simplicity is expressed at the end of 2 Timothy 2:13, where we learn that God cannot deny himself.

Spiritual

God does not have a physical body. He is a spiritual being. As Jesus explained to the Samaritan woman at the well, "God is spirit" (John 4:24). Angels are also spiritual beings, but they are creatures. Only God is a *divine* spiritual being. On certain occasions God miraculously took on some kind of visible and physical form. For instance, he appeared in the form of a man to Abraham (in Gen 18 compare vv. 2, 8 with vv. 10, 13; also v. 16 with vv. 17, 20, 22). However, occasions like this are exceptions that God makes for a special purpose. In his very own nature God is spiritual.

Eternal

Time began when God started to create. Scripture starts with these words: "*In the beginning* God created the heavens and the earth" (Gen 1:1). This is confirmed shortly after that when we read, "And there was evening, and there was morning, the *first* day" (Gen 1:5). As a result, everything other than God has a beginning and is both temporal and time-bound. This includes even such basic things as matter itself, light, and energy. Only God is eternal. He has no beginning and no end (Ps 90:2); he is not subject to time but, rather, sovereign over time. He can stop time (Josh 10:12–14), and he can even reverse time (2 Kings 20:8–11).

Incomprehensible

We can know God since he has revealed himself, but we cannot *completely* comprehend, or fathom, who he is or how he works. For more details on what is called the incomprehensibility of God, see chapter 4.

Invisible

God is spirit (see *spiritual*, above). Since he does not have a physical body, he is also invisible to our natural, human eyes. "No one has ever seen God" (John 1:18; see also 1 Tim 6:16). It is true that in Exodus 24:10 the Holy Spirit says that Moses, Aaron, Nadab, and Abihu, as well as the seventy elders "saw the God of Israel." However, we must understand this as one of those special occasions at which God appeared in some kind of visible form. By nature, however, he is still invisible.

Immutable

Literally, the immutability of God means that he does not change. Some people have the mistaken idea that this implies that he does not move, act, empathize, or grieve. They suppose that God is like a divine statue enthroned in a heavenly but stony stoicism. Clearly, this is not the God who reveals himself in Scripture. God grieves deeply and he has a tender heart of compassion (Gen 6:6; Hos 11:1–4, 8). He acts to defend his people (Exod 15:1–21). So, *immutable* does not mean *immobile*. Instead, it describes how God is steadfast and consistent in his plans and actions (Ps 33:11; Mal 3:6; Jas 1:17). God does not say one thing and then do another. If he plans it, he does it. If he announces it, he accomplishes it. Even on those occasions when God does relent from a punishment that he had threatened to impose (Exod 32:14), he remains consistent with his own character and compassion (Exod 34:6–7).

Infinite

With human beings, there is always a limit. We reach the limit of our mental capacity. At the end of a hard day of work, we also come to the end of our physical strength and stamina. We become exhausted. With

God there are no such limitations. His understanding is limitless (Job 11:7–9); his strength never runs out (Isa 40:28). Therefore we must be careful never to think of God in a limited, creaturely manner. Unlike us, he is infinite.

Almighty

There are two aspects to God's almighty power. On the one hand, he is more than sufficiently strong to do whatever he chooses to do. He can make the noonday sun stop shining (Luke 24:44–45), or he can bring the dead back to life (1 Kings 17:22). These are things which are simply impossible for us, but they are possible for God because he is almighty (Luke 1:37). On the other hand, *almighty* also expresses the fact that God governs over all (Rev 4:8; compare with 5:13–14). In other words, God is almighty with respect to both his *power* and his *position*.

Wise

Wisdom is more than knowledge. Wisdom is knowing the right thing to do at the right time and in the right way. God is not only infinite in his knowledge, he is also perfect in his wisdom. This is evident in creation. One look at a flower or an animal, and the words of the psalmist come to mind: "O LORD, how manifold are your works! In wisdom have you made them all" (Ps 104:24). Evidence of God's wisdom can also be found in the salvation that he has worked for us in Jesus Christ. Which human being would ever have thought up the plan to save sinners by sending God's eternal Son to be born from a virgin and then to die on a cross? Human beings would never have come up with such a plan! Many have even ridiculed it as nonsense. Yet it is a most glorious display of God's wisdom (1 Cor 1:18–31).

Just

Without fail, God always knows the difference between good and evil. Even Satan recognizes that (Gen 3:5). Furthermore, God not only knows the difference between good and evil, he also takes action against those who are guilty of sin, and he punishes the evildoer (Exod 34:7). In this way God himself is just and administers justice to others. God does not need a law outside of himself in order to determine whether something is right or wrong. God intuitively knows right from wrong, and therefore he himself determines what is right and what is wrong. Then, in order to teach us about his just requirements, he has revealed his righteousness in his law (Ps 119:137; Isa 42:21).

Holy

Closely linked to God's justice is his holiness. *Holy* means *set apart, distinct*. God is holy in two senses. First, with respect to his nature and being, God is distinct from all creatures, and he is, of course, radically set apart from all false gods (Exod 15:11). Second, with respect to morality, God is set apart from and opposed to all that is sinful, wicked, impure, and unclean (Hab 1:12–13).

Good

The Belgic Confession says that God is good in himself, and that he also generously gives good gifts, like a fountain of fresh water that keeps bubbling to the surface (Ps 135:3; Jas 1:17). In his goodness God takes diligent care of his creation (Pss 104:27–28; 145:9), even being generous toward those who do not believe in him (Matt 5:45).

Gracious

God's graciousness is closely related to his mercy, compassion, and patience. It describes his forgiving love and faithful kindness toward sinners who do not deserve or merit them in any way (Titus 3:4–5). For this reason we often speak of God's sovereign grace. The addition of the word *sovereign* emphasizes that the basis of God's grace lies entirely within himself, and not within us (2 Tim 1:9). It is helpful to distinguish between God's goodness, which he extends toward all people, and his grace, which he showers upon his chosen ones (see chapter 12 for more detail).

In the last few decades it has been popular in some circles to speak about the openness or vulnerability of God. This trend is also called *open theism*. Open theists usually begin by affirming that God exercises general rather than meticulous providence. In other words, they believe that God has a general plan in mind for the direction in which he wants history to go, but he does not control all the little details of what happens from day to day. Then they often continue by saying that God has purposefully restricted his own sovereignty and knowledge in order to give human beings room to co-operate with him in determining the course of history. Practically speaking, this means that God does not know everything about the future, and God will sometimes change his mind on the basis of what human beings decide to do. In short, open theists believe that God is open toward the future and can even be surprised by developments that take place.

Now that we have studied the perfections of God, it should be clear that open theism must be rejected. To begin with, the Lord reveals himself to be the God of meticulously complete providence, even to the point that he knows how many hairs there are on your head (Matt 10:30) and determines whether a sparrow lives or dies (Matt 10:29). Also, God's eternal plan and purpose includes everything (Eph 1:10–11). Nothing catches him by surprise.

However, more is at stake. Open theism makes God less infinite and more finite, less immutable and more unpredictable. In short, it makes God more like a human being. Open theists take this approach because they are afraid that speaking about an almighty, immutable God makes him sound too cold and impersonal. However, if we remember that simplicity is one of God's perfections, then this problem is resolved. God is as compassionate as he is almighty; he is as loving as he is immutable. None of God's perfections compromises the other ones. Indeed, God's glory shines through all the more brightly when we confess that he is *both* infinitely almighty *and* immeasurably gracious.

Suggested Reading: Exodus 3

QUESTIONS FOR UNDERSTANDING

1. Summarize the meaning of God's personal name, Yahweh, or I AM
    WHO I AM. What benefits do Christians receive from knowing the
    name of their God and applying its truth to their daily lives?
2. Read Psalm 110 and Mark 12:35–37 carefully. Using what you
    have learned about God's names and titles, especially *LORD* and
    Lord, explain how Jesus Christ's argument works.
3. God is eternal, and we are promised "eternal life" (Matt 19:29). Are
    God's eternity and our eternity the same? Explain your answer.
4. Explain how God's justice and mercy are simultaneously displayed
    in the same Saviour, namely, Jesus Christ. Article 20 of the Belgic
    Confession will be helpful.

QUESTIONS FOR FURTHER DISCUSSION

1. Read Jonah 3. On the one hand, God announces through his prophet
    that Nineveh will be destroyed in forty days (v. 4). On the other
    hand, we read that God did not destroy the city (v. 10). How does
    this fit with God's perfection of immutability?
2. God is invisible and "no one has ever seen or can see" him (1 Tim
    6:16). That being the case, what does the apostle John mean when
    he writes that "we shall see him as he is" (1 John 3:2)? Does this
    "him" refer to God the Father (v. 1) or God the Son (v. 2) or both?
    Will our glorified eyes be able to do something that our present eyes
    cannot do? Or will this be a different kind of seeing, e.g., some kind
    of spiritual seeing? In your discussion also refer to Job 19:26 and
    Matthew 5:8.
3. Some people struggle with the combination of God's eternity and
    immutability. They say, "Since God is eternal, he knows the past,
    the present, and the future. In the morning God already knows what
    is going to happen to me in the afternoon, and he is not going to
    change his mind. So, why should I even pray to God? It's all a
    foregone conclusion." How would you respond to someone who is
    having this struggle? Lord's Day 45 will be also helpful.

4. On the basis of James 1:17 the Belgic Confession describes God
    as the "overflowing fountain of all good" (Art 1). Yet someone
    will surely make the following observation: "There are many things
    which flow from God's hand that are anything but good: war,
    disease, floods, and hurricanes." This leads to the obvious question:
    how can bad things flow from a perfectly good God? How would
    you answer that question?

CHAPTER 6.

FATHER, SON, AND HOLY SPIRIT

One evening, as a father is tucking in his child for the night, his seven-year old son says, "Dad, may I ask you a question?" "Of course," replies the father. The son asks, "Why do we talk about God as Father, Son, and Holy Spirit, when there's only one God? It makes it sound like he is three gods." Patiently the father explains, "No, he is one God, but at the same time as being one God, he is also three persons. That is why he is called the triune God." To this the son replies, "I know, Dad, I've heard that word *triune* before. But it still does not make sense to me. Either God must be one, or he must be three, but he cannot be three and one at the same time, can he? According to the rules of math, that does not work. One plus one plus one equals three, not one!"

Do you understand what the seven-year old boy is struggling with? Not only children but also adults have a hard time understanding the doctrine of the Trinity. According to elementary math, one plus one plus one equals three. So, logically, if we speak of Father, Son, and Holy Spirit, then we should also speak about three gods. Yet the Bible is very clear that the LORD is one (Deut 6:4). What are we to make of this? How are we to think about it?

Since the doctrine of the Trinity is hard to understand, many Christians do not draw from it as much spiritual strength and comfort as they should. They may well believe it, but they do not frequently *use* it. In their minds this doctrine is mostly something that theologians will discuss and debate. However, not only theologians need this doctrine; all Christians do. In the first place, it is part of true faith. True faith accepts all that God has revealed in his Word (LD 7), and Scripture does reveal a triune God (see the next section below). Therefore, even if it is hard to understand, it is crucial that we believe it. You can think back to what we learned about faith and the limits of human understanding in chapter 4.

Secondly, the early church devoted a lot of energy to making sure they confessed this doctrine correctly. The Apostles' Creed, the Nicene Creed, and the Athanasian Creed all deal explicitly, and sometimes extensively, with our triune God. If it was so important for the early church, it should also be important to us today.

Thirdly, one of the most significant events in a Christian's life is his or her baptism. Baptism is administered in the name of the Father and of the Son and of the Holy Spirit. Baptism also ought to be used throughout our lives to strengthen our faith (see LD 25, Q&A 65). So, through our baptism the teaching about our triune God becomes a very personal and profitable doctrine.

GOD HAS SO REVEALED HIMSELF IN HIS WORD

In Lord's Day 8, Q&A 25, the Catechism asks, "Since there is only one God, why do you speak of three persons, Father, Son, and Holy Spirit?" In other words, the Catechism understands quite well the question that the seven-year old son asked his father. Our logic cannot fathom exactly how God can be three-in-one. Surprisingly, though, the Catechism's answer is short and to the point. In fact, the answer is only one sentence. Also, it does not bring forward various analogies in creation to give us some limited understanding of the Trinity. For example, many have said that the Trinity can be compared to a triangle: three points, yet one shape. But the Catechism does not use such analogies. Instead, it simply states: "Because God has so revealed himself in his Word that these three distinct persons are the one, true, eternal God." In short, the Catechism is saying this: God describes himself as triune, and if anyone knows who God is, then surely it is God himself!

We must also remember that God is God; he is not a creature. Often the reason that we struggle with this doctrine is that we are still thinking about God in a far too human manner. Among human beings it is certainly true that if you have three persons, then you have three human beings. Three persons do not make one human being! However, what applies to creatures does not necessarily apply to the Creator. We must be careful that we do not—intentionally or unintentionally—pull God down to our level.

Let us turn to the Bible now and see how God reveals himself as triune, starting with the Old Testament. The first two verses of the Bible already teach us something about the Trinity. On the one hand, it is clear that there is only one God. Scripture begins with these words: "In the beginning *God* created the heavens and the earth" (Gen 1:1). It does not say "gods" but one "God." But in the very next verse we read that "the Spirit of God was hovering over the face of the waters." This raises some questions. Is the Spirit of God in verse 2 the same as God the Creator in verse 1? Is there any kind of distinction between the two? At this point, so early in Scripture, these questions are not yet answered. However, the LORD reveals more as his Word progresses.

The next revelation of God's triune nature is in Genesis 1:26. There God speaks on the sixth day of creation. Just as in Genesis 1:1, it is one God—not gods—who is speaking. Yet he speaks in an unexpected way. He says, "Let *us* make man in *our* image, after *our* likeness." Now, since there is only one God speaking, we would have expected him to say, "Let *me* make man in *my* image, after *my* likeness." However, even though he is the one God, he speaks using plural pronouns. This is not a one-time occurrence either. The same pattern is repeated in Genesis 3:22 and, later on, in Genesis 11:6–7. At this point, the LORD still has not revealed many details. He speaks in the plural, but he has not revealed *how many* persons he is, or what their names are. But there is more revelation to come.

One of the first indications that God is Father comes in Exodus 4:22. The LORD sends Moses to say to Pharaoh, "Then you shall say to Pharaoh,

'Thus says the LORD, Israel is my firstborn son.'" By implication this also means that the LORD is Israel's Father. Likewise, in Hosea 11, the LORD speaks passionately about Israel as his child, calling him "my son" (v. 1) and describing how he taught Israel to walk, leading him with "cords of kindness" (v. 4), and refusing to give up on him and abandon him because, after all, he was his very own child (v. 8).

Moreover, what is implicit in Exodus 4 and Hosea 11 becomes explicit in other passages. For example, in Deuteronomy 32:6 Moses rebukes the Israelites by asking, "Do you thus repay the Lord, you foolish and senseless people? Is not he your father, who created you, who made you and established you?" Similarly, in Jeremiah 3:19, the LORD directly admonishes his people when he says, "And I thought you would call me, My Father, and would not turn from following me." There are also other places in the Old Testament where the LORD speaks of himself as the Father, including Isaiah 63:16 and Malachi 2:10. In sum, then, God reveals himself as the Father who loves his children with a strong and compassionate love. Understandably, he is also deeply offended when his people, who are his very own children, turn their backs on him and forsake him.

At the same time, already in the Old Testament, it is clear that there is more to the LORD than being Father. There are certain occasions when we hear about a special Son. When this particular Son is described, we can only come to one conclusion: he is God. For example, in Psalm 2 the LORD makes a decree saying, "You are my Son, today I have begotten you" (v. 7). This Son will rule over the entire earth (v. 8), and all people, even kings, are summoned to "kiss the Son" (v. 12), just as much as they are called to "serve the LORD with fear, and rejoice with trembling" (v. 11). Thus, at the end of Psalm 2 the Son is put on par with the Father.

This becomes even clearer in Psalm 110 where David calls one of his own sons "my Lord" (v. 1). As Jesus explained to the Jews in Mark 12:35–37, the only way to understand this psalm correctly is to acknowledge that this particular son of David is also, and at the same time, God. What is deduced from Psalm 110 is made explicit in Isaiah 9:6, where the prophet announces, "For to us a child is born, to us a son is given; and the government shall be upon his shoulder, and his name shall be called Wonderful Counsellor, Mighty God, Everlasting Father, Prince of Peace." On the one hand, this Son of whom Isaiah speaks is to be human, since he will be born. Yet, on the other hand, he must also be God. Otherwise why would he be called "Mighty God"? Likewise, Daniel 7 speaks of a "son of man" who rides on the clouds of heaven and rules over all people of every nation. These are clearly divine privileges. In short, then, as the Lord continues to reveal himself in Scripture he teaches us that he is not only Father but also Son. Moreover, in the Old Testament it is prophesied that this Son who is God will also be a son of man, that is, a human being. These prophecies were fulfilled at the incarnation of God's eternal Son (John 1:14).

Finally, the Holy Spirit is also revealed in the Old Testament, starting with Genesis 1:2, as we saw above. However, it does not stop with the first chapter of the Bible. Frequently we hear about the Holy Spirit descending upon certain individuals, especially prophets, kings, and judges (Num 11:17; Judg 3:10; 6:34; 1 Sam 16:13, etc.). Lest anyone think that the Spirit of God is only some kind of divine force, the prophet Isaiah says that the people of Israel "rebelled and grieved his Holy Spirit" (Isa 63:10). Grieving is something that is done with respect to a person, in this case a divine person, the third person of our triune God.

Clearly, the LORD was busy throughout the Old Testament revealing himself as the one, true, and triune God. These revelations become even clearer in the New Testament. Two passages immediately come to mind: Matthew 28:19 and 2 Corinthians 13:14. In Matthew 28 the Lord Jesus Christ sends out his apostles with these words: "Go therefore and make disciples of all nations, baptizing them in the name of the Father and of the Son and of the Holy Spirit." He speaks of one name (not names in the plural) and yet he refers to three persons. This verse is perhaps the most clear and succinct revelation of our triune God. This is also confirmed at the end of 2 Corinthians, when the apostle Paul gives his final greeting and blessing: "The grace of the Lord Jesus Christ and the love of God and the fellowship of the Holy Spirit be with you all." Understanding God in this verse to refer to God the Father, we once again hear all three persons mentioned side by side. Other passages that teach about the Trinity are:

God the Father: Matthew 6:25–34; John 5:16–27; Romans 8:12–17.

God the Son: John 5:26, 8:58; Colossians 1:13–20; Hebrews 1:3, 5–14.

God the Holy Spirit: John 14:16–17; Acts 5:3–4; 2 Corinthians 3:17–18.

In addition, the Belgic Confession gives a helpful summary of these passages in Articles 8–11.

We have taken only a brief look at some of the key passages in which the LORD reveals himself to be triune. Even from this short survey it should be evident, however, what a rich and full doctrine it is. Not only do we have a God who is the loving Father who cares for all creation, and especially his children, but this same God is the Son who became man and worked redemption for us, and he is the Spirit who dwells in our hearts, shaping and moulding us to be more and more like our Saviour (LD 32). When we think about the Trinity, we should not think of a doctrine that is confusing but, rather, one that is truly comforting. What a blessed thing it is to be baptized in the name of this triune God. It is triple blessedness. It is an indescribable privilege *three times over*!

THE IMPLICATIONS OF CONFESSING ONE GOD

Now that we have looked in Scripture at how God reveals himself to be triune, it is good to analyze the implications of this doctrine. Not all, but many false religions are polytheistic, that is to say, their followers believe in the existence of many different gods. The ancient religions of Canaan, Egypt, Babylon, Greece, and Rome were all characterized by the worship of many gods. Typically, there would be gods of war, fertility, health, and wealth. In many religions the sun, moon, and stars were worshipped as gods. Often dead ancestors were also worshipped and given some kind of divine status. Also in the world today there are polytheistic religions: Hinduism, Buddhism, and neo-paganism, of which Wicca is one kind.

Since it confesses one God (Deut 6:4), the Christian faith immediately sets itself apart from all belief in many gods. This also affects the character of Christian worship. In polytheistic religions the gods often compete, or even fight, with each other. Moreover, even in those polytheistic religions that have a more peaceful pantheon, the worshipper is busy trying to make sure he keeps all the various gods happy. If a worshipper starts to neglect a particular god, it may well happen that this god becomes angry with him and makes his life difficult. By contrast, in the Christian faith we do not have to worry about frantically running after all kinds of different gods, trying to divide our worship time equally among them. Rather, we worship one God, and we know that we have a good standing before him, only by faith for the sake of Jesus Christ (LD 23).

At the same time, because the three persons—Father, Son, and Holy Spirit—are completely united as one, we never have to worry that there might be some tension or misunderstanding among them. As Jesus Christ said, "I and the Father are one" (John 10:30). The three persons have always worked together in perfect and seamless harmony, and they will always continue to do so. This, too, is a great blessing for us.

THE IMPLICATIONS OF CONFESSING THREE PERSONS

The Christian faith is most certainly a monotheistic faith. This means that we worship only one (*mono*) God (*theos*). At the same time, it is different from other monotheistic religions, such as Islam. Other monotheistic religions tend to believe in a more impersonal god. God is described in them as the Almighty, the Sovereign, the Supreme One, or something similar. However, the God of Holy Scripture is, first of all, Father. By its very nature, *Father* is a personal and relational term. God is also Son, and *Son* is a very personal and relational term. Finally, God is also Spirit. At first glance, *Spirit* may not seem to be as personal as *Father* or *Son*. However, when we consider that in Scripture the Spirit hovers with care (Gen 1:2), is grieved by rebellion (Isa 63:10; Eph 4:30), groans in the prayers of God's children (Rom 8:26), and serves as the Counsellor for the church until the return of Christ (John 14:15, 26), then it is clear that the Holy Spirit does not in any way diminish but, on the contrary, increases how personal God is. So, the three persons, who are the one God, ensure that God is not the cold, distant, impersonal god of deism (see chapter 5) or other monotheistic religions.

At the same time, it has always been challenging to find just the right way of describing the relationships among the Father, Son, and Holy Spirit. In particular the early church devoted a lot of time to this issue. Consider, for example, these excerpts from the Athanasian Creed:

> Now this is the catholic faith, that we worship one God in trinity and trinity in unity, without either confusing the persons, or dividing the substance. For the Father's person is one, the Son's another, the Holy Spirit's another; but the Godhead of the Father, the Son, and the Holy Spirit is one, their glory is equal, their majesty is co-eternal.

> The Father is from none, not made nor created nor begotten. The Son is from the Father alone, not made nor created but begotten. The Holy Spirit is from the Father and the Son, not made nor created nor begotten but proceeding. So there is one Father, not three Fathers; one Son, not three Sons; one Holy Spirit, not three Holy Spirits. And in this trinity there is nothing before or after, nothing greater or less, but all three persons are co-eternal with each other and co-equal.

The Athanasian Creed is careful to maintain equality among all three persons. At the same time, the creed is equally diligent not to confuse any of the three. Each person remains distinct, yet fully united as one God. In this way the distinctiveness of the three persons is not compromised or cancelled out by the truth that God is one.

Now you may wonder if this level of doctrinal detail is required of all Christians. Or can this kind of precise theological language about the Trinity be left up to the experts in theology? This question is perfectly understandable; however, the answer may be surprising to some. The Athanasian Creed ends by saying, "This is the catholic faith. Unless a man believes it faithfully and steadfastly, *he cannot be saved.*" In other words, something eternally important is at stake here for all believers. But why?

To explain this further, the Athanasian Creed was written to refute a man named Arius (A.D. 256–336). Although he spoke of the Son as a god, Arius taught that Jesus Christ was some kind of lesser god. This teaching is also called *subordinationism*, a term which is another way of saying that some people make Christ out to be someone less than true and complete God. However, as soon as anyone compromises the full divinity of Jesus Christ, he also compromises the heart of the gospel. Our salvation depends upon having a deliverer who is both true God and true man—fully God and fully man (LD 5–6)! Without that, we are without hope. So, since the heart of the gospel was at stake, the Christians in the early church went to great lengths to make sure that the doctrine of the Trinity was accurately and fully confessed. If it were anything less than that, we would still be stuck in our sin and misery.

JEHOVAH'S WITNESSES AND MORMONISM

The teachings of Arius are still alive today. Both the Jehovah's Witnesses and the Mormons teach that Jesus Christ is a god, but they add that he is a lesser divine being than the Father is.

During the latter part of the nineteenth century and the early part of the twentieth century, the Watch Tower Society, commonly known as the Jehovah's Witnesses, slowly grew and became organized. Charles Taze Russell and Joseph Franklin Rutherford were two key founding fathers. Today this organization has approximately eight million members and can be found throughout the world. They are well known for distributing tracts and magazines from door to door.

The Church of Jesus Christ of Latter-day Saints, also known as the Mormons, is a large organization as well. It has some fifteen million members worldwide. Founded by Joseph Smith in New York State, it now has its headquarters in Salt Lake City, Utah.

Both the Jehovah's Witnesses and the Mormons corrupt the gospel precisely on the point of who Jesus Christ is. They both teach that he is a divine being. For them Christ is more than just a normal or average human being. But both deny that Christ is truly and fully God, even as the Father is God. However, Scripture is clear: the Word, who is Christ, is God—true God of true God (John 1:1, 14). Moreover, it is exactly this truth that, as we said above, qualifies Christ to be our only Mediator and Deliverer (Rom 1:1–4; LD 5, 6). With a Saviour who is truly God we have a salvation that is truly and eternally effective. In the end, then, confessing our triune God is not a confusing riddle; instead, it is a very rich comfort!

Suggested Readings: Psalm 110; Matthew 28:16–20

QUESTIONS FOR UNDERSTANDING

1. Explain how John 8:58–59 demonstrates that Christ is God. In this connection you will find it helpful to review the discussion of the name *Yahweh,* or I AM WHO I AM, in chapter 5.
2. Explain how Acts 5:3–4 demonstrates that the Holy Spirit is God.
3. Using books that you have available to you or online resources, describe how the Muslims view God, whom they call Allah. How does the Muslim view of God differ from the view of God as revealed in the Bible? Can you think of three specific points of difference?
4. Find a copy of the Athanasian Creed. Read through the entire creed. Take note of any words or phrases that you do not understand. Discuss these as a group and try to clarify the meaning together.

QUESTIONS FOR FURTHER DISCUSSION

1. Many Reformed churches use an official liturgical form when baptism is administered. Below is a quotation from such a form. Discuss at least three different ways in which this explanation could help Christians in their daily walk of life.

When we are baptized into the name of the Father, God the Father testifies and seals to us that he establishes an eternal covenant of grace with us. He adopts us for his children and heirs, and promises to provide us with all good and avert all evil or turn it to our benefit.

When we are baptized into the name of the Son, God the Son promises us that he washes us in his blood from all our sins and unites us with him in his death and resurrection. Thus we are freed from our sins and accounted righteous before God.

When we are baptized into the name of the Holy Spirit, God the Holy Spirit assures us by this sacrament that he will dwell in us and make us living members of Christ, imparting to us what we have in Christ, namely, the cleansing from our sins and the daily renewal of our lives, till we shall finally be presented without blemish among the assembly of God's elect in life eternal.[1]

2. Organizations such as the Jehovah's Witnesses and the Mormons will often say that the doctrine of the Trinity was developed later by the church, in the third and fourth centuries, but that it is not found in Scripture itself. How would you respond to this challenge?

3. What is the best way to explain the doctrine of the Holy Trinity to a seven-year old child? Would you use analogies such as the triangle (i.e., three angles, yet one shape) or time (i.e., past, present, and future, yet one chronology)? Or do those analogies hinder rather than help?

4. When sharing the gospel with those who are unfamiliar with it, at what point would you introduce the doctrine of our triune God? Is it something that should wait until they have become quite familiar with other scriptural teachings? Or is it such a foundational doctrine that you need to bring it up sooner rather than later?

---

1. *Book of Praise: Anglo-Genevan Psalter* (Winnipeg: Premier Printing, 2014), 597.

CHAPTER 7.

OUR FATHER AND HIS CREATION

"In the beginning God created the heavens and the earth" (Gen 1:1). It is with this well-known sentence that the Bible begins. On the one hand, it is both short and simple. The words and phrases are not complicated or confusing. The time of the action is indicated: "in the beginning." The one who did the action is identified: "God." And finally, what he did is described: he "created the heavens and the earth." On the other hand, this sentence is deeply profound. It also raises questions. Who precisely is this God who creates? What is he like? And what motivated him to create something entirely new?

In addition, many more questions have been raised, particularly concerning the relationship between faith and science. Many, but not all, scientists believe that all living beings, from small fish to human beings, evolved over long periods of time. To be more precise, these scientists teach that through the processes of adaption and natural selection simpler life forms (such as jellyfish and crayfish) eventually evolved into more complex life forms (such as blue whales and human beings). These processes require a long time span of millions upon millions of years. Genesis 1 and 2 provide an undeniably different explanation of how our present world came into existence. This revelation from God says that creation occurred over the course of six days. Furthermore, it did not happen through constant adaption but rather through divine command. God spoke, and it came to be (Ps 33:9). So, which is correct? Creation by God's Word? Or evolution through adaptation? Or is some combination of the two possible? Just to be clear on terminology, this attempt to find a hybrid solution is often called theistic evolution.

Many sincere Christians struggle with these questions. As children they grow up learning from the Bible that God simply created everything in six days. Yet later on, in high school and university or through personal reading, they receive a different impression from scientific research. For some it becomes a crisis of faith. So, also for their sake, we must not avoid these important questions, and we will not do so. We will deal with them a little later on in this chapter.

However, first we must pay attention to something else. When the early church confessed God's work of creation, they emphasized that God *the Father* is the Creator. This is clear from the Apostles' Creed, which begins, "I believe in God the Father almighty, Creator of heaven and earth." Please note that the confession of God as the Father is prior to the confession of God as the Creator. That order is not accidental, and it is confirmed by the Nicene Creed, the Heidelberg Catechism (LD 9), and the Belgic Confession (Art 12). Each creed or confession emphasizes, right from the start, that the God who creates is the Father. We will heed the wisdom of our forefathers in the faith and follow the same direction. There are many people in this world who acknowledge that there is a God or a higher being, but they do not know, trust, and love him as Abba (Gal 4:6). Also for their sake, we need to speak clearly about God as Father.

GOD THE FATHER IS THE CREATOR

The consistency with which the creeds confess God the Father as Creator is all the more noteworthy when we consider that each age has had its own scientific theories concerning how things are and how they came to be. The Apostles' and Nicene Creeds were written in a time that was still heavily influenced by Greek philosophy. Philosophers such as Aristotle (384–322 B.C.) and Ptolemy (ca. A.D. 90–168) held different scientific views, both with respect to the arrangement of the heavens and the constitution of the earth. However, the Apostles' and Nicene Creeds do not touch on such matters; rather, they point to the Creator who is almighty Father.

Likewise, some twenty years before the Belgic Confession and Heidelberg Catechism were written, Nicolaus Copernicus was causing waves in the scientific and theological communities of his day. He proposed that the sun, rather than the earth, was at the centre of the celestial spheres. The theologians at that time were certainly aware of Copernicus' new ideas. In fact, a Lutheran theologian named Andreas Osiander wrote the preface to Copernicus' famous book, *On the Revolution of the Celestial Spheres* (1543). Yet again, the authors of the Belgic Confession and the Heidelberg Catechism do not spend time addressing these views. Instead, they are keen to confess that God *the Father* is the Creator. Why is this confession so important?

In the first place, it is crucial because it is biblical. The prophet Malachi says, "Have we not all one Father? Has not one God created us?" (Mal 2:10). The same truth is revealed in the New Testament when the apostle Paul writes, "Yet for us there is one God, the Father, from whom are all things and for whom we exist, and one Lord, Jesus Christ, through whom are all things and through whom we exist" (1 Cor 8:6). This last verse also makes it clear that all three persons of our triune God are involved in creation. The Father creates; he is the source. However, as the apostle Paul points out in 1 Corinthians 8:6, the Father creates through the Son. Indeed, the apostle John writes, "All things were made through him, and without him was not any thing made that was made" (John 1:3). Also, no sooner was the first act of creation completed than the Holy Spirit was immediately active, taking care of the waters that had been made (Gen 1:2; also see Ps 104:30). Clearly, each person of our triune God participates in the creation and maintenance of the heavens and the earth. It remains true, however, that God the Father is the one who is central in this doctrine.

Secondly, we need to ensure that we understand correctly *why* God is called Father. Let us begin by clarifying that he is not called Father because he is the Creator. If that were the case, then God would have only *become* a Father on the first day of creation. Now, of course, when we speak about earthly fathers, this is what we are used to. A boy grows up to be a man. If a man is married, then he becomes a husband. If the Lord blesses that marriage in such a way that the couple receives a baby, then, and only then, the husband *becomes* a father. However, it is also entirely possible to be a man and not be a father. In other words, being a father is something that is added to, but not essential to, being a man. The same cannot be said of God the heavenly Father. He did not become a Father. He always was, is, and forever shall remain Father because he is the eternal Father of his eternal Son, Jesus Christ (2 Cor 1:3; LD 9). This truth brings with it a most remarkable stability and security. God's Fatherhood is simply part of who he is. It is not something that was added into his existence, and it cannot be taken away either. Another way of saying this is that God can never stop being Father nor stop being fatherly. If he were to do so, he would be denying himself, and that is something God will never do (2 Tim 2:13).

Thirdly, confessing God as Father brings the purpose of his creative work into sharper focus. To be sure, the final and highest purpose of God's creative work is to bring glory to his name. The apostle Paul makes this explicit when he exclaims, "For from him and through him and to him are all things. To him be glory forever. Amen" (Rom 11:36). However, it is also true that as Father, God keeps in mind the needs of his children, whom he loves so much (Matt 6:26, 32). God the Father always had his eternal Son, whom we now know as Jesus Christ. Yet on the sixth day of creation he made two earthly children for himself, namely Adam and Eve. (We will look more closely at that aspect of creation in chapter 9.) Therefore all the other things that he created on the first six days had a clear purpose: they all had to serve, help, and assist his children. To say it in another way, God the Father not only *cares for* his children, he also *created for* his children.

In the fourth place, since he is Father, God has a particular view of everything that he created. He does not merely look at the mountains, rivers, stars, animals, and human beings as things that he made, as if they were nothing more than an inventory of products in a universe-sized warehouse. No, creation has a much more elevated status than that. In his paternal eyes they are all part of the inheritance that is set aside for his eternal Son. Psalm 2 speaks of this truth, especially in verses 7–8. There the psalmist writes, "I will tell of the decree: The Lord said to me, 'You are my Son; today I have begotten you. Ask of me, and I will make the nations your heritage, and the ends of the earth your possession.'" This is also confirmed in Hebrews 1:2, where the Holy Spirit speaks of the Son whom God the Father appointed heir of all things, that is, of the sum total of all created things.

Closely connected to this is the astounding truth that God the Son also graciously shares his inheritance with all those who are regenerated by the Spirit of God. This is revealed in Romans 8:16–17: "The Spirit himself bears witness with our spirit that we are children of God, and if children, then heirs—heirs of God and fellow heirs with Christ, provided we suffer with him in order that we may also be glorified with him." And on the final day, when the Lord brings all his children into the new creation, they will enjoy their inheritance forever, in unspeakable and uninterrupted glory: "And he who was seated on the throne said, 'Behold, I am making all things new' . . . . The one who conquers will have this heritage, and I will be his God and he will be my son" (Rev 21:5, 7). Notice again how cosmically sweeping this promise is. Our inheritance includes the entire renewed creation. So, the next time you look at a blossoming flower, a gurgling brook, or a twinkling star, remember: it is not only a beautiful part of creation, but it is also part of your promised inheritance, through Christ, the eternal Heir of the heavenly Father.

Considering all the points above, it is obvious that our ancestors in the faith were on the right track when they emphasized that God the Creator is the eternal, loving, wise, and almighty Father. This truth sheds a profound and comforting light upon the whole doctrine of creation.

OUT OF NOTHING

God the Father is the Creator, not the Sculptor, of the heavens and the earth. In other words, God did not take pre-existing, eternal matter and re-shape it into the heavens and the earth. On the contrary, there was nothing—except God. Then God spoke and one by one, day by day, he brought the various parts of creation into existence. It is true that as God's creation work progressed he did use some things that he had created earlier in the week in order to create something else. The heavenly Father used dirt and dust to create both animals (Gen 1:24) and Adam (Gen 2:7). He also used a rib from Adam's side to create Eve (Gen 2:21–22). Still, when God the Father began his work of creation, there was nothing for him to begin with.

This truth is taught in Scripture in various ways. To begin with, Genesis 1:1 does not speak of God using any pre-existent matter when he created the heavens and the earth. Rather, as Psalm 33:9 confirms, "He spoke, and it came to be; he commanded, and it stood firm." Moreover, the apostle Paul explains that God is the one who simply "calls into existence the things that do not exist" (Rom 4:17). In the book of Hebrews we are exhorted to believe that our heavenly Father does have the power to create something out of nothing: "By faith we understand that the universe was created by the word of God, so that what is seen was not made out of things that are visible" (Heb 11:3). The confessions also make a point of mentioning this significant truth (BC 12; LD 9).

The full significance of this truth becomes apparent if we set it next to the doctrine of God's eternity. Since God created the heavens and the earth, in the beginning and out of nothing, all matter is finite and time-bound; it all has a definite beginning point. By contrast, God has no beginning; he, and he alone, is eternal. In Psalm 90:2 Moses sings, "Before the mountains were brought forth, or ever you had formed the earth and the world, from everlasting to everlasting you are God." Since God is eternal and all creatures are not, there is a sharp line of demarcation between the two—a line that we do well to maintain.

A number of false teachings blur the boundary line between Creator and creature. The most extreme of these teachings is *pantheism*. Pantheism teaches that ultimately everything is God. This means that the mountains, the moon, the animals, and all human beings are divine, although their divinity is manifested in different ways. Religions such as Hinduism and Buddhism, as well as many mystical religions, have elements of pantheism in them. For instance, in Hinduism Brahman is divine, and "everything is Brahman."[1] Obviously, the sharp demarcation line between Creator and creature is erased entirely.

A closely related teaching is *panentheism*. Followers of panentheism do not assert that God is everything, but rather that God is *in* everything, or conversely, that everything is *in* God. However, this only raises the question: to what extent is everything in God? And if something is completely in God, does this not make everything divine again? In the final analysis, is panentheism so much different from pantheism? Whatever the correct answer may be to that question, the fact remains that panentheism makes the boundary between Creator and creator very blurry.

Finally, there is *materialism*. Although there are different forms of this teaching, some variations teach that matter as such, including atoms, is eternal. As a result, materialism affirms two eternals: God and matter. Naturally, atheistic materialism denies the existence of God altogether and maintains that only matter is eternal. Yet either way matter takes on an eternal status, which should be the exclusive claim of God alone.

In each of the three teachings outlined above, the line of demarcation between Creator and creature is compromised. The inevitable result is that God becomes more creaturely, or the creature becomes more divine, or both. However, Scripture clearly maintains that the Creator is not in the same category as his creation. As the LORD himself says, "To whom then will you compare me, that I should be like him?" (Isa 40:25–31). This truth has at least one very crucial consequence: it protects the uniqueness of the incarnation of Jesus Christ. Both pantheism and panentheism teach that it is a rather normal thing for divinity and humanity to be combined or conjoined. According to these teachings, such a combination is simply part of the way things naturally exist. The holy gospel has a radically different and infinitely better message. When the Word, who is God, became flesh (John 1:1, 14), a most unique and miracu-

1. Vedas, *Chandogya Upanishad* 3.14.1.

lous event took place. Our very salvation depends upon that miracle (LD 5–6)! In this way we are also reminded that the doctrines of the Christian faith are intricately interconnected. Making a mistake in the doctrine of creation also has big repercussions elsewhere, including the doctrine of salvation.

ALL THINGS VISIBLE AND INVISIBLE

The Apostles' Creed simply states that God created the heavens and the earth. The Nicene Creed expands on this by adding a phrase: "all things visible and invisible." Why should we be interested in things that we cannot even see? And what exactly is this invisible realm anyway? To be specific, the invisible realm includes the angels who serve the Lord as well as those angels who have rebelled against the Lord, otherwise known as evil spirits or demons (2 Pet 2:4; BC 12). Angels and demons are spiritual. They do not have physical bodies, although at times they do appear in a visible form that is similar to a human being (compare Gen 18:2, 22 and 19:1).

Since angels are spirits who normally dwell in the heavens (Luke 2:13–15), it easily happens that people tend to put them in the same category as God himself, or at least they think of them as demi-gods. But they are wrong in doing so. Angels, like human beings, are creatures. Angels are not eternal. Angels are not almighty. Angels had a definite beginning and, like all other creatures, they must ultimately submit to the Creator. This truth is comforting for God's children, especially when they consider that Satan is a fallen angel (Job 1:6; Jude 6). Satan is opposed to God, but he is definitely not equal to God. Satan's counterpart is not God but the loyal archangel Michael (Rev 12:7–9). Consequently, even though Satan is a roaring lion who attacks us with many enticing temptations and deceiving schemes, as God's children we can be confident that, in the end, God our Father will be victorious. If the contest is between the Creator and a creature, between the infinite One and a finite being, the eternal Creator will win every time. Satan will, most assuredly, go down to total defeat (Rev 20:7–10). Since our Father is God, and Satan is not, there is no doubt about it!

IN SIX DAYS

The first week of world history was undoubtedly a most special and unique week. At the beginning of the first day there was nothing. By the end of the sixth day God the Father had created the heavens and the earth, complete with water, light, weather systems, continents, trees, flowers, sun, moon, stars, birds, fish, mammals and, last but not least, human beings. So much accomplished in so little time! It was truly miraculous. Let us be honest, it is impossible for anyone of us to wrap our minds fully around that miracle. In fact, the enormous scope of what the Lord did in that special week has led some to question whether it all really happened in just one week. Some have suggested that the mention of days in Genesis 1 may, in fact, be a poetic way of referring to much longer periods of time, perhaps even millions of years.

It is true that the word *day* can be used in a more metaphorical sense, referring to a period of time. For example, Proverbs 25:13 speaks about snow in the time of harvest. Literally, the word *time* is *day*, but harvest takes longer than one day. Yet, even if *day* can refer to a longer period of time, there are three key reasons for maintaining that this is not the case in Genesis 1. First, in Scripture whenever the word *day* is used with any kind of number (e.g., first, second, or forty days), it always refers to a literal, historical day.

Second, Genesis 1 contains a well-known refrain: there was evening and there was morning, the first day . . . the second day . . . the third day, etc. However, that is not the only time the word *day* is used in this chapter. It is also found in verse 14, where we learn that God created the sun, moon, and stars to be "for signs and for seasons, and for days and years," and again in verse 18, where the celestial lights are "to rule over the day and over the night." It is clear, and no one really disputes this, that in those two verses the word *day* is not used in a metaphorical or poetic sense but refers, rather, to ordinary days as we know them today. Therefore, if *day* is used in its normal sense in verses 14 and 18, we should fully expect that it is used in the same way in verse 19, which mentions "the fourth day," as well as in the other five occurrences of that well-known refrain.

Thirdly, in the fourth commandment the LORD himself draws a clear and close parallel between the six days that we work each week and the six days that he worked to create all things in the beginning. In Exodus 20:9–10, he commands, "Six days you shall labour and do all your work, but the seventh day is a Sabbath to the LORD your God." Then, in verse 11 he bases this command on the creation week: "For in six days the LORD made heaven and earth, the sea, and all that is in them, and rested on the seventh day. Therefore the LORD blessed the Sabbath day and made it holy." Put together, these two facts give sufficient reason for maintaining that our heavenly Father created the heavens and the earth, including all things visible and invisible, in six literal and historical days. It may be impossible for us to comprehend how he did it all, but what is impossible for man is possible for God (Matt 19:26).

Since he is the God of order (1 Cor 14:33), it is not surprising that his creative work is also organized. On the first day God created light. On the fourth day he made light-bearers: the sun, moon, and stars. On the second day God created an expanse to separate the waters above and the waters below. On the fifth day he filled the waters below with fish and the expanse above with birds. On the third day God created the dry land with many different plants and trees. On the sixth day God filled that land with all kinds of animals and human beings. Thus, there is a clear pattern of forming (days 1–3) and filling (days 4–6). This pattern does not indicate that Genesis 1 is a poetic or metaphorical chapter of the Bible. It simply confirms that our Father, the Creator, is an organized Master Designer.

CREATION, EVOLUTION, THEISTIC EVOLUTION

The theory of evolution is based on various scientific discoveries and data. In this section we can highlight only a few. Geologists have discovered patterns in the layers of rock. As they found certain kinds of fossils in certain layers of rock, geologists slowly worked on piecing together a history of the development of life by analyzing the patterns they found in these rock formations. Then there are also the striking similarities between certain creatures. Monkeys, apes, and gorillas all share many of the same physical features. This has led scientists to ask if one species evolved from the other. Indeed, this question has been extended to the similarities between apes and human beings. Developments within molecular biology, especially DNA research, have confirmed that ninety-six percent of the genomes are the same in humans and chimpanzees.

Of course, it is one thing to collect data. It is another thing to interpret those data. How should we interpret the fact that humans and chimpanzees share ninety-six percent of their genomes? Those who believe in evolution cite it as proof that evolution occurred. Those who believe in creation will say that God the Creator obviously had a well thought out, effective design for living creatures. Rather than making each living creature genetically unique, God re-used elements of his design work in various creatures. Even human architects will borrow elements from previous blueprints when they design a new building.

However, there is a more fundamental issue at stake here. We already touched on it in back in chapter 2. Whenever we study parts of creation, whether rock layers or DNA patterns, we are receiving some general revelation. As the apostle Paul explains, general revelation teaches something about who God is: how powerful he is, how wise he is, and how divine he is (Rom 1:20). But general revelation is limited in what it can reveal (CoD 3/4.4). Therefore, in order to learn clearly and correctly how God created the heavens and the earth, we need to rely on special revelation, that is, Holy Scripture. Moreover, Scripture does not speak about evolution by constant adaption, but creation by divine command.

This also highlights another key weakness with the theory of evolution. Whatever insights the theory may offer, it does not provide a satisfactory explanation as to how life actually began. Proponents of evolution all acknowledge that there must have been an epoch-altering event in which inorganic, lifeless material suddenly began to live. Still, it is one thing to suggest *that* lifeless material began to live, but it is quite another to explain *how* this happened. So long as the theory of evolution leaves that question unanswered, it has failed to truly address the issue of origins, despite claims to the contrary.

As mentioned earlier, the attempt to combine creation and evolution is called theistic evolution. This theory maintains that evolution is the means by which all living beings eventually came into existence. However, theistic evolution adds that God is the one who initiated the whole process as well as the one who directed it. The idea of theistic evolution must be rejected for two main reasons. First, in his Word, the LORD does not speak anywhere of using a process of evolution. True faith is accepting what God reveals (LD 7), and our Father has revealed that "he spoke, and it came to be" (Ps 33:9). Secondly, all proponents of evolution, whether theistic or atheistic, teach that death is simply part of the way that things naturally are. For them, death is a necessary part of the process of natural selection, otherwise known as survival of the fittest. The Lord clearly reveals, however, that death entered the world because of sin (Gen 2:17; Rom 5:12, 17; Rom 6:23). Therefore Christ also had to die on the cross as the only satisfaction sufficient to pay for sins (Matt 16:21). Once again, we notice that it is crucially important to have the correct doctrine of creation; otherwise many other areas of doctrine, including the very heart of the gospel, that is, Christ's death on the cross, may well become diluted or corrupted.

In short, since evolution is such a common teaching today, it can be challenging for us as Christians to take a different stance. We may even be mocked as being scientifically backwards or ignorant. In answer to that, there is also excellent science being done that questions evolution and supports creation. Yet more than that, it comes down to trusting our Father the Creator and what he says to us in his Word. Who can better tell us how he performed the miracle of creation than the Master Designer and Maker himself?

Suggested Readings: Genesis 1; Hebrews 11:1–3

QUESTIONS FOR UNDERSTANDING

1. Explain the significance of confessing that God has always been Father, even before the creation of the world. Can you think of

concrete situations in which this truth would be comforting to
God's people? How so?

2. Define pantheism, panentheism, and materialism. Can you think of
   world religions, popular movements, or contemporary authors who
   promote these ideas? Also, try to think of examples that are not
   mentioned in this chapter. What are at least two fundamental errors
   that these teachings promote?

3. We often speak of ourselves as children of God, but we do not often
   take the next step and think of ourselves as heirs of God. What
   exactly does this mean? What is all included in our inheritance? Is
   it spiritual, physical, or both? To find your answers consider the
   following passages: Romans 4:13; Galatians 4:1–7; Ephesians 1:11,
   14, 18; Titus 3:7; Hebrews 11:7; James 2:5; Revelation 21:5–7.
   Being an heir includes not only privileges but also responsibilities.
   What are they, and how must we fulfil them? Consider Romans
   8:17.

4. Compare the first heavens and earth as they were before the fall
   into sin (Gen 1–2) and the new heavens and earth (Rev 21–22).
   What is similar? What is different? How do these similarities and
   differences comfort us and challenge us?

QUESTIONS FOR FURTHER DISCUSSION

1. What tasks do angels have? (Gen 32:1, 2; Matt 4:11; Luke 16:22;
   Heb 1:14). Are certain angels assigned to particular people in order
   to protect them from physical harm? What about spiritual harm?
   (Matt 18:10).

2. Are we overly concerned about the spiritual forces of evil, that
   is, Satan and his demons? Or insufficiently aware and concerned?
   How do we take our stand against the devil's schemes without
   seeing a demon behind every difficulty in life? Ephesians 6:10–18
   may help in your discussion.

3. Sometimes people are perplexed by the fact that God created light
   on the first day (Gen 1:3), whereas he created the sun on the fourth
   day (Gen 1:14–16). Logically, one might expect that God would
   create the sun, as a source of light, before the light itself. Yet God

took a different approach. What theological significance might this have? Looking at texts such as Joshua 10:12–14, Matthew 27:45, and especially Revelation 21:22–25 may help you.

4. Concerning the origin of this world and human life, Christians sometimes say that the Bible tells us one thing and scientific discoveries tell us another thing. They feel caught between the two. They do not want to contradict the Bible, but neither do they want to dismiss scientific data casually. How can Christians work through this? What advice would you give?

CHAPTER 8.

OUR FATHER AND HIS PROVIDENCE

Our heavenly Father, who created all things, also takes care of them all. Every day again he makes sure that the entire universe keeps running. As if that were not enough, in addition to maintaining it all, he governs the affairs of all his creatures so that ultimately they serve his plan and purposes. In one word we call this God's *providence*.

Now, the interesting and at times perplexing truth is that we often respond differently to God's creation as compared to his providence. The same heavenly Father is responsible for both, yet our reactions to his works can be quite dissimilar. For example, we see the delightfully delicate petals of a vibrantly colourful flower and we praise our Father for it. We tickle a baby, listening for the gleeful giggles that erupt from his little lungs, and we are amazed at how the Father has designed human beings. When we behold the vast beauty and intricate precision with which our Father made all the stars in the galaxies, we respond with awe and wonder.

Yet when we analyze the same Father's work of providence, especially how he governs the affairs of our lives, we often react in a different manner. We have many questions. A child who is nine years old may die of cancer, but the child's great-grandmother who is ninety years old continues to live. Why, Lord? Floods and tornados destroy homes and businesses; they also kill men, women, and children. Why, Lord? Drought cuts the harvest in half, when the economy is already suffering. Why,

Lord? Concerning God's providence we have many questions and also a few doubts. We might even be tempted to think that if only we, human beings, were in charge, then we would govern things in a better and more prosperous way. But it is precisely for this reason that we must hold the doctrines of creation and providence together and remember that the same wise and loving Father is responsible for both.

To be sure, there is an important difference between creation and providence. Creation took place in the first week of world history and it was finished after that (Heb 4:3, 4). By contrast, our Father's work of providence is ongoing. Every day again, he maintains what he made. Yet, without denying this difference, we must also be careful to hold the doctrines of creation and providence closely together. In fact, God himself already reveals this connection in the first two verses of the Bible. Genesis 1:1 speaks of the doctrine of creation: "In the beginning God created the heavens and the earth." At the same time, we read in Genesis 1:2 that "the Spirit of God was hovering over the face of the waters." This teaches us about providence. The Spirit of God was hovering over the waters to take care of them, even as an adult eagle might hover over its young eaglets, carefully watching over them as they learn to fly (compare Gen 1:2 with Deut 32:10, 11). So we can say that God's work of providence began already on the very first day. Providence started before creation was finished.

The Heidelberg Catechism also maintains a close link between creation and providence. For example, Lord's Day 9 is about God the Father our Creator. Yet right in the middle of Answer 26 about creation we read that God "still upholds and governs [all things] by his eternal counsel and providence." Similarly, even though Lord's Day 10 is about God's providence, Question 28 asks, "What does it benefit us to know that God has created all things and still upholds them by his providence?" With this in mind let us explore further the doctrine of providence and the deep comfort that is part and parcel of it.

The Word of God assures us that the heavenly Father provides his children with many good things. The most well-known passage that gives this assurance is Matthew 6:25–34. There Jesus Christ builds a simple but powerful argument. In the first place he points to the birds. These winged creatures do not keep a large Tupperware container full of food in their nests, do they? And yet every day they have food to eat. Who feeds them? Jesus Christ answers, "Your heavenly Father feeds them" (Matt 6:26).

Two things are noteworthy in this answer. First, Jesus Christ points to *the Father* as the provider. Second, he does not say "their Father," referring to the birds, or "my Father," speaking of himself, but rather "*your* Father," indicating that the Father focuses on the needs of those who trust in him. Actually Christ makes this explicit as he continues, "Are you not of more value than they?" In other words, surely the Father takes care of his own children before tending to all the other responsibilities he may have. He then repeats the same kind of argument, only this time he uses the example of wild lilies. So, the next time you begin to worry about this or that, have a look for a bird or take a glance at a flower. Just as the heavenly Father is taking care of them, so he will certainly take care of you, too, according to your needs (Matt 6:31–33).

Similarly, the apostle James reminds us, "Every good gift and every perfect gift is from above, coming down from the Father of lights with whom there is no variation or shadow due to change" (1:17). Now, without a doubt, if our Father always and only gave us good and perfect gifts, then there would be fewer questions in our minds and less doubt in our hearts. Wouldn't you agree that providence would be a much easier doctrine to comprehend if there were no such thing as suffering or sickness? But as we all know, there are also many difficult things that happen in this world. These adversities happen to unbelievers, but they happen to believers as well.

Do difficult and painful things come from exactly the same hand as the good and perfect things? At times this seems hard to accept. However, according to Lord's Day 10 both rain and drought, fruitful and barren years, health and sickness, riches and poverty, come to us, not by chance, but by his fatherly hand. This raises an urgent question, however. A loving earthly father would never want to give his child sickness or poverty. In fact, he would do everything within his power to prevent his child from going through those hardships. So how can it be that the loving heavenly Father at times does give sickness, poverty, or other difficulties to his children? Doesn't this seem to go directly against the grain of what it means to be a father?

When we discuss the doctrine of providence, it is very tempting to let our minds run away and rapidly reach all kinds of logical conclusions. For example, it might be tempting to conclude that if the heavenly Father gives one of his very own children a sickness, then obviously he is not a very loving Father. But we need to restrain our eager minds and redirect them toward God's revelation.

A good place to start is Hebrews 12. It is clear that the recipients of the letter to the Hebrews were going through hard times. In verse 4 we read, "In your struggle against sin you have not yet resisted to the point of shedding your blood." In other words, they were not martyrs (yet), but they had endured other forms of persecution such as insults and imprisonment (Heb 10:32–34). Still, the Holy Spirit says that the fatherly hand of God has been involved in all of this as well. He continues by saying, "It is for discipline that you have to endure. God is treating you as sons. For what son is there whom his father does not discipline? . . . Besides this, we have had earthly fathers who disciplined us and we respected them. Shall we not much more be subject to the Father of spirits and live?" (Heb 12:7, 9). The point is this: hardships are never pleasant, and some are extremely painful; however, in the end, they can still serve a good purpose. As God's Word says, "For the moment all discipline seems painful rather than pleasant, but later it yields the peaceful fruit of righteousness to those who have been trained by it" (Heb 12:11).

Our heavenly Father can give hard things to his children and remain loving. However, in order for us to understand this, we need to focus on what our suffering can produce over time, not just on how painful it is at the moment. In fact, the apostle Paul even goes so far as to say that we can even rejoice in them, "knowing that suffering produces endurance, and endurance produces character, and character produces hope, and hope does not put us to shame, because God's love has been poured into our hearts through the Holy Spirit who has been given to us" (Rom 5:3–4; also see Jas 1:2–4). Undoubtedly we can all agree that these words are easy to read but hard to apply.

Still, our heavenly Father's perspective is always so much broader and farther than our limited insight. From his hand we may receive a sickness in our bodies. This frustrates us, but our Father may well be teaching us patience and trust in him. In other words, he is focusing on the health of our soul at the very same time that our minds are occupied with sickness of our body. It may also be the case that the Father puts us through an aggravating and disappointing time in our life. Through it he builds perseverance and character in us (Rom 5:4). In addition, since he knows the future, our heavenly Father may well be preparing us for a later time in our life when there will be an even greater difficulty to face, and we will need that perseverance and character which he cultivated in us earlier on. Alternatively, he may give us a bitter hardship so that through the trial fellow believers learn to pray for the one who suffers, to help him, and to think less about themselves and more about those in need. Finally, in adverse times our God often gives us prime opportunities to evangelize and testify about the light of God's grace in the darkness of life's valleys. These are but a few examples of how the broad and long-term vision of the Father does work, in love, for the good of his children.

Still, all believers find it hard at times to trust wholeheartedly that "for those who love God all things work together for good" (Rom 8:28). Some things? Yes. Most things? Perhaps. But *all* things? That is hard to believe. However, the antidote to this doubt is no one less, and no one else, than the Saviour Jesus Christ himself. Those chosen to be God's children are God's children only for the sake of Christ (LD 13). This also means that when the Father looks at his adopted children, he looks at them through his eternal Son, Jesus Christ.

Would the eternal Father work for the ill or demise of those who belong to his much beloved Son? Of course not! Indeed, the apostle Paul phrases it even more strongly than that: "He who did not spare his own Son but gave him up for us all, how will he not also with him graciously give us all things?" (Rom 8:32). Therefore, "I am sure that neither death nor life, nor angels nor rulers, nor things present nor things to come, nor powers, nor height nor depth, nor anything else in all creation, will be able to separate us from the love of God in Christ Jesus our Lord" (Rom 8:38–39). In short, since believers belong to Christ, and since the Father loves his only-begotten Son, believers can also be assured that God the Father loves them, and that nothing can take the Father's love away from them.

GOD IS ALMIGHTY BUT NOT THE AUTHOR OF SIN

In a sense we have already dealt with this topic in chapter 5 when we considered the perfections of God, which included his almighty sovereignty. But it is good to expand on this briefly. A false teaching called *deism* promotes the idea that once God was finished with creation, he pulled back and became something like a heavenly spectator who only watches the show below. Scripture teaches differently. Our Father is sovereign over all the inanimate parts of creation, such as the weather patterns (Job 38:22–30, 34–38) and the star constellations (Job 38:31–33). He rules over all the different kinds of animals (Job 39:1–30). He is the supreme Governor over all nations, from Chile right through to Cambodia and beyond (Ps 99:1–3). He also rules over the invisible realm, over both the angels who serve him willingly (Ps 103:20–21) and the demons who rebel against him (Luke 10:17). Even Satan ultimately has no choice but to submit to God's decrees (Job 2:6–7; Rev 12:9, 12).

The scope of God's providence extends to the small and seemingly insignificant details of life as well. If a hair falls from your head, or a little sparrow dies, it does not happen randomly; instead, these events are planned by God (Matt 10:29–30; Luke 21:18). This all-inclusive providence gives us an immense security and stability in life since, as explained above, Romans 8 assures us that nothing in all creation can separate us from God's love. However, there are also those who see a negative side to such a comprehensive providence. They are concerned that if God governs every detail of life, then human beings become little more than robots who execute the divine program that God has downloaded into their brains. At the same time, they suggest that if God's providence is all-inclusive, then humans are no longer responsible for their actions, and consequently God becomes responsible for human sins. For this reason, advocates of open theism propose a limitation on God's providence (also see chapter 5). They teach that God controls the general direction of world affairs but does not involve himself in the smaller details of daily living.

How shall we answer this challenge to the truth of Scripture? Is the Father of lights really the author of sin? Once more, the first step is to return to God's own Word. Two examples will suffice. The first is from Genesis, in the account where Joseph's brothers sold him as a slave to the Midianite merchants (Gen 37:12–36). It is clear that the brothers had sinful motivations for their actions. They were jealous of their brother Joseph. They were also angry about his dreams, which indicated that one day Joseph, though younger, would be superior to his older brothers. Driven by jealousy, anger, and greed, they therefore sinned against God and against Joseph by selling their sibling into slavery. These brothers could not, and should not, blame God for their actions. As the apostle James explains, they were not tempted by God. Rather, they were tempted when they were dragged away by their own evil desires, desires which started small but swiftly grew to malicious maturity (Jas 1:13–15).

Clearly, Joseph's brothers were responsible and accountable for their own sins. Yet God was involved in these events as well. Years later, when Joseph was re-united with his extended family and his father had died, his brothers became worried that he would take revenge on them. On that occasion Joseph said, "As for you, you meant evil against me, but God meant it for good, to bring it about that many people should be kept alive, as they are today. So do not fear; I will provide for you and your little ones" (Gen 50:20–21). In other words, Joseph's brothers, who sinned against him, were responsible for their evil deeds. They were *not* unaccountable robots. At the same time, by his providential power, God the Father was working in and through that sinful situation for a much better and grander purpose.

Another example can be found in the book of Job. When the Chaldeans formed three raiding parties and stole all of Job's camels, they were clearly motivated by greed (Job 1:17). Their action was a direct transgression of the eighth commandment. Yet, at the same time, God was active in this situation for a completely different purpose. As the LORD reveals earlier in this chapter, Satan had cast doubt upon the sincerity of Job's faith. But the LORD planned to prove, beyond any doubt, that the faith that he had worked in Job's heart was sufficiently genuine to endure horribly agonizing trials (Job 1:6–12). In line with this, when tragedy after tragedy strikes Job, he confesses, "The LORD gave, and the LORD has taken away; blessed be the name of the LORD" (Job 1:21). It remains true that the Chaldeans were the ones who grabbed Job's camels and ran away with them. Yet, on another level, Job's confession is also correct: "The LORD has taken away." The Chaldeans intended it for evil, but the LORD planned it for good.

To sum up, then, God the Father is more than capable of governing over sins, and even turning evil toward good purposes, without ever being, or becoming, the Author of those same sins. As God, he can easily take the mud of iniquity and turn it into pottery that is useful for his purposes, all the while keeping his hands and his heart spotlessly free of all evil. The most brilliant example of this uniquely divine capability is Jesus Christ's death by crucifixion. Surely, Christ did not deserve to be crucified. Surely his condemnation was the greatest legal injustice ever done to anyone—in this case to a man who was entirely innocent and free from all sin (Heb 4:15). Yet, miracle of miracles, out of this shocking injustice God brought forth an unspeakably great salvation for all those who put their trust in the Christ. It may be foolishness in the eyes of the world, but if we look at it with the eyes of faith, we stand amazed at the wonder of God's wisdom (1 Cor 2:18–31).

God is sovereign also over wicked deeds, without becoming tainted by those sins. This is revealed in Scripture, but it is admittedly hard to understand. In fact, our human minds do not have the capacity to fathom the depths of God's providential ways. In Article 13 the Belgic Confession makes quite a point of this. After affirming that "in this world nothing happens without [God's] direction," it goes on to say:

> Yet God is not the Author of the sins which are committed nor can he be charged with them. For his power and goodness are so great and beyond understanding that he ordains and executes his work in the most excellent and just manner, even when devils and wicked men act unjustly. And as to his actions surpassing human understanding, we will not curiously inquire further than our capacity allows us. But with the greatest humility and reverence we adore the just judgments of God, which are hidden from us, and we content ourselves that we are pupils of Christ, who have only to learn those things which he teaches us in his Word, without transgressing these limits.

Simply put, there is a God-ordained roof over our heads. Everything that the heavenly Father teaches us in his Word we can, and we should, study eagerly. However, when we reach the limit of his revelation, we must rein in our curiosity; otherwise we are guilty of trespassing into God's own territory. The only thing gained by attempting that impertinent feat is a big goose egg and a bad headache from repeatedly banging our heads on the divinely ordained ceiling.

Now it is helpful to return to the tight connection between the doctrines of creation and providence. There are many things about the way God designed his creation that we simply do not understand (Job 38–41). To give but one example, who understands every detail of how a baby is formed in his mother's womb (Ps 139:13–18)? Likewise, we simply do not understand many things about our Father's providential governing. Why does our Father allow one to fall sick and another to stay healthy? How does he use disasters such as tsunamis and tornados to accomplish his good purposes? Often we cannot (fully) answer these *why* and *how* questions. But there is a more important question, the *who* question.

Whatever the circumstance may be, we always know who is firmly in control: our heavenly, loving Father, the Creator of heaven and earth. As the Belgic Confession explains at the end of Article 13, this is a great comfort:

> This doctrine gives us inexpressible consolation, for we learn thereby that nothing can happen to us by chance, but only by the direction of our gracious heavenly Father. He watches over us with fatherly care, keeping all creatures so under his power that not one hair of our head—for they are all numbered—nor one sparrow can fall to the ground without the will of our Father. In this we trust, because we know that he holds in check the devil and all our enemies so that they cannot hurt us without his permission and will.

OUR HEAVENLY FATHER USES ORDINARY MEANS

Since God *can* do miracles, some people expect that he *must* do miracles, and that he must do them when they desire or ask. For example, there are good number of preachers today who will tell you that if you just trust enough in God, he will make you healthy and he will make you wealthy. Sometimes people call this the health and wealth gospel. Conversely, these preachers often suggest that if you do not receive health or wealth, there must be something wrong with your faith. Perhaps you need to pray more, believe more strongly, or live a holier life.

Such a message simply does not line up with what God reveals. Job became very sick (2:7), even though he was a blameless and upright man (1:1). The apostle Paul left Trophimus sick in Miletus (2 Tim 4:20). Even the apostle Paul himself was left with some kind of physical ailment, although he had prayed earnestly that the Lord would take it away from him (2 Cor 12:7–10). Moreover, when Timothy was not feeling well, the apostle Paul did not tell him to pray more or believe harder. He simply told him to include some wine in his diet, a remedy which can help with certain stomach ailments (1 Tim 5:23).

Concerning wealth, the Lord's instructions are quite clear. The apostle Paul directs the Thessalonians as follows: "We urge you . . . to aspire to live quietly, and to mind your own affairs, and to work with your hands, as we instructed you, so that you may walk properly before outsiders and be dependent on no one" (1 Thess 4:11). In his second letter to the church at Thessalonica the apostle uses even stronger language. Concerning those walking in idleness, he writes: "Now such persons we command and encourage in the Lord Jesus Christ to do their work quietly and to earn their own living" (2 Thess 3:12). Please notice the common theme in these passages. It is not *pray and become a millionaire*, but rather *work for your daily bread.*

God's providence does not mean that we should avoid our duties. We need to take good care of our bodies, and when we become ill, we can certainly make use of the medicines and other medical treatments that are available to us. Similarly, we need to work diligently to earn an income and provide for the basic daily needs of our families. It remains true that God can still act in surprising and even extraordinary ways, restoring health when the doctors are unable to do anything more or providing financial resources from the most unexpected sources. However, the key thing to remember is that we may not demand these things from our Father in heaven. As a Father, God provides according to his wisdom, not necessarily according to our desires or agendas, let alone our fickle wishes and whims. Just as children often do not perceive the wisdom of their earthly parents until they grow up themselves, so also we may have to wait until the life hereafter to appreciate fully the wisdom of our heavenly Father's providence in this present life.

Suggested Readings: Job 1:13–22; James 1:12–18

QUESTIONS FOR UNDERSTANDING

1. Give one similarity and one difference between creation and providence. Also, explain why they are significant.
2. It is comforting to know that the heavenly Father has all things in his sovereign hand. At the same time, the apostle Paul adds that "in him [that is, Christ] all things hold together" (Col 1:17). What exactly does this mean, and how does it add to our comfort?
3. When healthy parents have children who are seriously ill, they often

struggle to understand the Lord's ways. They feel that if anyone should be so sick, it should be they, for they are much older. Using what you have learned about providence in this chapter, what would you say to parents in such a situation?

4. Are sicknesses or other hardships necessarily a sign of God's disfavour? If we become sick, how should we think about it from a spiritual perspective? Can sickness ever be a sign of God's judgment? John 9:1–5, 1 Corinthians 11:30, and 2 Corinthians 12:9–10 will help you formulate an answer.

QUESTIONS FOR FURTHER DISCUSSION

1. Here is a scenario to consider: A devout Christian young lady is having trouble. She has just lost her job, although she worked very hard. Her fiancé has broken off their relationship, although she tried to be kind and loving toward him. On top of that, her unbelieving parents are blaming these hardships on her Christian faith. This sister is often praying, "Why, Lord?" and she does not feel that her question has been answered. What comfort can you give her? How should she respond to her parents?

2. Why were there so many miracles in the days of prophets such as Moses, Elijah, Elisha, and, of course, our Saviour Jesus Christ? Do miracles still happen today? What exactly is a miracle? How extraordinary does it need to be before it "qualifies" as a miracle? Is surviving a serious car crash truly a miracle, or should we reserve this term for events like the healing of a paralytic or the raising of the dead?

3. Here is another scenario to consider: A married couple is struggling to make ends meet, financially speaking. They have been praying about it. One day the husband comes home all excited because a mining company in northern Canada contacted him unexpectedly and offered him a job with nearly double the salary he presently receives. He says to his wife, "Don't you see it? It's the answer to our prayer. God has providentially opened up a door that we did not even know about." But moving up north would take them far away from both family and church. How far can we go in saying

that providential events are God's way of saying "Do this" or "Stop that"? Is God's providence equal to God's revealed will for our lives? Deuteronomy 29:29 will help.

4. Are there ever situations in life when a Christian is left with no choice but to sin? To say it in another way, can God's providence lead one of his children into such a dire situation that, whichever way he turns, he sees no other option than to commit a sin? Try to come up with a situation or two in which that might seem to be the case and then work with 1 Corinthians 10:10–13 and James 1:13–15 to answer the question.

CHAPTER 9.

CREATED IN THE IMAGE OF GOD

If you could see as well as an eagle does, you could spot an ant moving on the ground from the highest balcony of a ten-storey building. If you could smell as well as a polar bear, you could sniff out a seal that was more than twenty kilometres away. If you had the stamina of a bar-tailed godwit, you could fly 11,000 kilometres from Alaska to New Zealand . . . non-stop!

Clearly, God has created animals which some truly extraordinary abilities. The more we learn about all these creatures with their diverse talents, the more we may be inclined to ask, "What is so special about human beings?" In answer to this question, people will often mention the intellectual and creative capacities of human beings. We may not have the eyesight and stamina of some animals, but we have figured out how to put a man on the moon. Besides, no animal ever composed the famous Ninth Symphony; a human being named Ludwig van Beethoven did. Others point out that human beings can communicate with language in a way that far transcends how even the chattiest parrot is able to do this.

However, if it is mental and linguistic abilities that set us apart, what about our fellow human beings who cannot think or speak very well, such as some of our mentally challenged brothers and sisters? Are they less human than we are? Clearly not. But then a question returns with even greater urgency. Among all the creatures that God has made, what is so special about human beings? The first chapter of Genesis provides a profound answer to this pressing question. On the sixth day, when God was just about to create Adam and Eve, the first two human beings, he said, "Let us make man in our image, after our likeness" (Gen 1:26). And it was so. "So God created man in his own image, in the image of God he created him; male and female he created them" (Gen 1:27). Three times in two verses the Holy Spirit emphasizes that human beings were created in God's image. Obviously the emphasis is purposeful. All of God's creative work fills us with awe and wonder. Yet with the creation of Adam and Eve something even more special happens. For unlike the birds, the fish, the livestock, and the insects, only human beings are created in God's image.

This truth demonstrates another difference between the revelation of Genesis 1 and the theory of evolution. Evolution is based on the premise that there is a fundamental continuum between animals and human beings. According to this theory, human beings have developed further than their animal ancestors, such as apes and chimpanzees. Human beings may stand straighter, think deeper, and communicate better, but there is nothing essential, or fundamental, that separates animals from humans. In this view it is always a matter of degree; the difference is seen as more quantitative than qualitative. However, in Genesis 1:26–27 the Lord reveals that there is a fundamental dissimilarity. All human beings are created in God's image; not even one animal is created in his image. This boundary remains today, and it must be maintained today.

All of this leads us to ask an obvious and necessary question: what exactly is this image of God? Is it simply and only an honour that God has given to us? Or is it some special capacity or ability that human beings have? Or is it a task that God has assigned to human beings? Or is it some combination of those three possibilities? We will seek to answer these questions in the next section.

THE IMAGE OF GOD: WHAT IS IT?

Over the centuries, theologians have defined the image of God in various different ways. As hinted at in the introduction to this chapter, one of the most popular explanations is that the image of God has to do with the special capacities of the human mind and will. The intellectual abilities of human beings are very impressive. Consider what men and women have all discovered and designed: efficient cars, increasingly fast computers, accurate GPS devices, splendid works of art, pleasing musical compositions, and effective surgical techniques. The list goes on and on. Surely, there is no other creature that even comes close to the mental acumen found in human beings!

Added to that, human beings make choices. They choose between one career and another, between one form of recreation and another, between one purchase item and another. This list also goes on and on. Whereas animals often seem to be driven by instinct, human beings evaluate their options and make informed choices. Therefore it is understandable that many theologians have pinpointed human intellect and choice as the key components of the image of God.

Closely related to this, but slightly different, is the idea that the image of God has to do with the capacity of human beings to have a relationship with God. If human beings could not talk or understand language, how could they communicate with God? Perhaps some kind of limited relationship could still exist, but God is one who speaks (see Gen 1), and therefore, if the relationship is to flourish, those who live with him also need to speak. Beyond this, it has been thought that since God is spirit (John 4:24), and since human beings have a soul, which is spiritual, there is a special contact point between God and human beings.

Other theologians emphasize that it is the triune God who said, "Let us make man in our image." In chapter 6 we looked at this remarkable aspect of Genesis 1:26. Since *one* God is speaking, we would expect him to say, "Let *me* make man in *my* image"; however, he says instead, "Let *us* make man in *our* image." Since it is the triune God who created man in his image, some have concluded that there should also be some kind of three-in-one aspect found in human beings. For example, the church father Augustine said that the human soul remembers itself, understands itself, and loves itself. So the soul has three distinct capabilities, but it is still one soul. This human "trinity" is said to be a reflection, or likeness, of the true, divine Trinity.

Finally, many theologians, especially from the Roman Catholic Church, make a distinction between *image* and *likeness*. They say that the image refers to the intellect and choice that God gave human beings, while the likeness corresponds to an extra gift that God gave to Adam and Eve, that is, their original righteousness and holiness. Simply put, for these theologians the image allows human beings to think and choose, while the likeness displays that they were created without sin.

So, what is the image of God? With theologians offering at least four different options, it might seem hard to answer this question in any definite fashion. However, the place to begin is to turn back to Scripture and listen carefully to what God reveals about this matter. The first thing that we should notice is that the creation of human beings in God's image is mentioned not only in Genesis 1:26–27 but also in Genesis 5:1–3. Let us look at the similarities and differences in these two passages.

> Then God said, "Let us make man in our image, after our likeness. And let them have dominion over the fish of the sea and over the birds of the heavens and over the livestock and over all the earth and over every creeping thing that creeps on the earth." So God created man in his own image, in the image of God he created him; male and female he created them.

> This is the book of the generations of Adam. When God created man, he made him in the likeness of God. Male and female he created them, and he blessed them and named them Man when they were created. When Adam had lived 130 years, he fathered a son in his own likeness, after his image, and named him Seth.

Both passages teach that God created man in his own image, in his likeness, and that he included both male and female in his image. However, the unique aspect of Genesis 1:26–27 is that God commands Adam and Eve to rule over creation. We will look at this more closely a little later on in this chapter. By the same token, Genesis 5:1–3 also has something special. It makes a connection between Seth, Adam, and God. Surprisingly, the relationship between Adam and Seth is described in terms of likeness and image (Gen 5:3), just as surely as the relationship between God and Adam and Eve is described using the same words (Gen 5:1; see also Gen 1:26). It is true that the Holy Spirit describes Seth as being in the image *of Adam*, whereas Adam was created in the image *of God*. We will come back to that detail in chapter 10 concerning sin. Nevertheless, the relationship between God and Adam is defined using the same words that express the relationship between Adam and Seth: image and likeness. For this reason we should link the image of God with a Father-children relationship.

This link is confirmed in the New Testament as well. The genealogy of Jesus Christ ends in a fascinating way (Luke 3:23–38). Slowly the genealogy works backwards, from one generation to the previous generation. At a certain point we reach Enosh, who is the son of Seth, who is the son of Adam, and we would expect the genealogy to stop there. After all, Adam is the first human being. He was formed from the dust of the earth (Gen 2:7). He has no ancestor, at least no earthly parents. Yet the genealogy of Luke 3 continues for one more step. In verse 38 we read, "Seth, the son of Adam, the son of God." Thus, the genealogies of Genesis 5 and Luke 3 help us make the important first step in defining the image of God. To be created in God's image means that, unlike all the rest of the creatures, Adam and Eve were created to be God's very own children.

Once we acknowledge the link between this Father-children relationship and God's image, it becomes clear why the word *likeness* is also used. Even in referring to the relationship between an earthly father and his child, we often use the expression *like father, like son*, or *like father, like daughter*. Children may speak, think, act, or even look in a way that is very similar to their father. Obviously, since God is spirit and human beings have a body, there is no physical resemblance between the two. However, when Adam and Eve were originally created, there were many other similarities between God and them. As God was righteous, so were they. The same applies to God's holiness, justice, and wisdom. All these divine attributes had a reflection, or likeness, in Adam and Eve. To be sure, God remained God, and Adam and Eve remained creatures. Yet, as

God's children, they reflected many of their Father's attributes in a manner that no other creature did. In the beginning, it was truly *like Father, like son and daughter*. This is summed up by the Heidelberg Catechism in Lord's Day 3 when it says, "God created man good and in his image, that is, in true righteousness and holiness."

This definition of God's image also helps us to appreciate the God-given dignity of human beings who are mentally handicapped. As we all know, there are people whose mental capacities are limited. Some of them cannot speak. Others cannot learn to do basic math equations, let alone design a computer. Still others cannot make simple choices such as whether to wear a red or blue shirt. Yet with conviction—and rightly so—we affirm that these special brothers and sisters are created in the image of God just as much as anyone else is. At the same time, this brings things into sharper focus. If God's image is primarily identified with the ability to think and choose, then people who have limited use of those capacities also have less of God's image. But if God's image is defined in the first place in terms of a Father-children relationship, then this is not a problem. Just as earthly parents say, "These *are* our children," regardless of whether one is a Rhodes scholar and the other is mentally challenged, so also the heavenly Father lays claim to all his children.

THE IMAGE OF GOD: WHY?

In the fifth commandment the LORD instructs children to honour their parents. This also applies in the relationship between the LORD and us. Since we, as human beings, were created in his image, and thus created to be his children, our primary purpose in life should be to honour our God. Various Scripture passages confirm this. In Proverbs 1:7 we learn that "the fear of the LORD is the beginning of knowledge." In this case, *fear* means *respect*. In other words, a person may claim to have all kinds of intelligence and understanding, but if he does not start from the point of honouring and respecting the LORD, then he has not yet made it to the starting line of true knowledge (see also Prov 9:10 and Job 28:28).

This theme becomes even stronger in the book of Ecclesiastes. There, at the end of his book, the Preacher makes the following concise and clear statement: "The end of the matter; all has been heard. Fear God and keep his commandments, for this is the whole duty of man" (12:13). In other words, someone may have big plans for his life. Beyond planning, he may even accomplish many great things: growing wealthy, becoming famous, and leaving a legacy behind after he dies. But if in all this activity he does not honour God or keep his commandments, all those labours are in vain. Such a person has missed the whole point and purpose of life for those who are created in God's image. To know the Father is eternal life (John 17:3), and to honour the Father is the highest purpose of life, both now and in eternity.

This should also help people who are struggling to find meaning and direction in their lives. Some feel that their lives lack meaning unless they have a certain career or job. Others seek significance in wealth. Still others feel they are worthless unless they have many friends. However, the doctrine of being created in God's image teaches us something different. Of course, it is good to have a fulfilling job, a steady income, and loyal friends. Yet even if someone has neither job nor money nor friends, if he but aims to respect God and obey his commands in everything, his life still has a definite purpose. In fact, such a life is pursuing the very highest goal that any human being could seek. As the Preacher says, "Fear God and keep his commandments, for this is the whole duty of man" (Eccl 12:13).

In addition to this primary purpose for all those created in God's image, there is also a secondary one. God expressed this in Genesis 1:26 when he said, "Let them have dominion over the fish of the sea and over the birds of the heavens . . . ." In other words, one of the key ways in which human beings can show respect for God is by taking good care of his creation. At the same time, this creation mandate has caused some concern. There are those who wonder if it does not leave the door open for people to abuse animals or other parts of creation, whether through neglect, malnourishment, harsh treatment, or pollution.

It is true that, ever since the fall into sin, people in power have often been corrupted by that power. History is full of examples of rulers who did not treat their citizens with kindness. Likewise, history is full of occasions on which human beings did not take proper care of other creatures. However, the mandate that God gave to Adam and Eve was not a licence to do whatever they pleased with God's creatures. Far from it! In Genesis 1:26 two important doctrines are revealed side by side. In the first place, there is the teaching about human beings being created in God's image (Gen 1:26a), and then, immediately thereafter, there is the command to rule over creation (Gen 1:26b). Although these two doctrines are not identical, they are inseparable. Being created in God's image, Adam and Eve were his children, and we might add, his royal children. God is the Creator who is King of kings and Lord of lords (1 Tim 6:15). Therefore, his children must be princes and princesses.

At the same time, then, in their ruling activity these children are obligated to reflect the good and wise government of their Father. Also in this regard it should be *like Father, like children*. As outlined in the previous chapter, God the Father governs all creation for good and wise purposes. In obeying the mandate of Genesis 1:26, human beings are to do the same. Abusing creation is not only a misuse of resources or animals; it is also an offence to the God who created them. Christians, of all people, should be highly motivated to take good care of the world that their heavenly Father made.

MALE AND FEMALE HE CREATED THEM

In Genesis 1:27 we read, "So God created man in his own image, in the image of God he created him; male and female he created them." A plain reading of this verse suggests that both men and women are created in God's image. In this respect they are equal. Also, both Adam and Eve are charged with the responsibility to take care of creation. The Lord clearly says, "Let *them* have dominion." He does not limit this command merely to Adam, in which case he would have said, "Let *him* have dominion." Even though this image was completely corrupted by the fall into sin, when this image is renewed by grace for the sake of Christ, the restoration applies to both male and female. The apostle Paul outlines this in Galatians 3:26–28, saying, "For in Christ Jesus you are all sons of God, through faith. For as many of you as were baptized into Christ have put on Christ. There is neither Jew nor Greek, there is neither slave nor free, there is no male and female, for you are all one in Christ Jesus."

Even though the teaching of Genesis 1:26–27 is quite straightforward, in the history of the church some people have questioned whether women were really created in the image of God. They did so on the basis of 1 Corinthians 11:7. Writing about proper decorum in worship, the apostle Paul says, "For a man ought not to cover his head, since he is the image and glory of God, but woman is the glory of man." At first glance this verse may indeed seem to indicate that only men are created in God's image. But if we read it carefully and pay attention to other related passages in the Bible, it is clear that women are certainly included in God's image. The first thing to notice is that 1 Corinthians 11 speaks about headship. For instance, in verse 3 the apostle writes, "But I want you to understand that the head of every man is Christ, the head of a wife is her husband, and the head of Christ is God." The last phrase is crucial. The head of the Son, Jesus Christ, is his eternal Father. The Son even submits to the Father and does his will (John 14:31). At the same time, the Father and the Son are equal in glory and dignity. In this regard the Son and the Father are one (John 10:3).

A similar sort of thing applies in the relationship between male and female. Women as well as men were created and are restored in the image of God. In this regard they are equal. However, *equal* does not necessarily mean *identical*. It is also true that God created Adam before Eve, and this divine order has certain practical consequences. The apostle Paul describes one of these consequences in 1 Timothy 2, where he teaches that, in the church, women may not have authority over men. The reason for this goes all the way back to creation: "For Adam was formed first, then Eve" (1 Tim 2:13). For this reason women should not serve as office-bearers who hold authority in the church.

Another consequence of this distinction is described by the apostle in the chapter to which we referred earlier: 1 Corinthians 11. In the church at Corinth some women were trying to look like men, especially in the way they cut and styled their hair (1 Cor 11:14–15). Also in our society there are women who try to look like men, and men who try to look like women. Any kind of androgynous look should have no place in the church of God, especially not in public worship. Rather than try to erase all distinctions between male and female, both in physical appearance and otherwise, we should affirm and celebrate the gender distinction. God has made men and women different, not only in their physical bodies, but also in their manner of dealing with issues and cultivating relationships. These differences do not make one gender more or less important than the other. On the contrary, they complement each other. Life is so much richer with two genders. The church would only impoverish herself if she tried to erase the differences between them.

THE IMAGE OF GOD AND THE FALL INTO SIN

In the next chapter we will deal more extensively with what Scripture teaches us about sin. However, it is fitting at this point to touch briefly on how the fall into sin affected the image of God. Did the image of God continue to exist in any way after the fall? Or was it completely obliterated by original sin?

The short answer to these questions is that God's image, though severely corrupted by sin, continues to exist after the fall. The most convincing proof for this is found in Genesis 9. This chapter records what the LORD said after the Great Flood. As the Holy Spirit makes clear, God sent that flood because man's sinfulness was so great (Gen 6:5, 6). After the Flood, sadly but undeniably, sin still existed, both in Noah's heart (Gen 8:21) and in his conduct (Gen 9:21). At the same time, though, in the midst of this post-Flood yet still-sinful world, God does refer to his image in human beings. In fact, he uses the presence of his image as a deterrent against further sin, especially the crime of murder. To be more specific, in Genesis 9:6 God says, "Whoever sheds the blood of man, by man shall his blood be shed, for God made man in his own image." Clearly, if God's image were completely eradicated by the fall into sin, this divine warning would have lost all of its weight. It would have become an empty threat.

At the same time, it should also be clear that God's image was drastically affected by the fall. Those who were created to be God's children now acted like insolent rebels. Those created to reflect their heavenly Father's likeness in righteousness and holiness now began to act more like the devil, embracing deceit, greed, and even jealousy that could explode into fratricide (Gen 4:1–16). Respect for the heavenly Father was replaced with violence and every form of evil inclination (Gen 6:5, 11–12). Obviously, God's image in man had been totally corrupted from every possible angle.

Yet there was a remnant among the ruins. Also today there is still the fact that God created human beings to be in a uniquely different category. Even if they act like irrational animals at times, God still deals with them as human beings. He expects human beings to respect and protect each other as those who were created in his own image, his own likeness. Furthermore, the image that was ruined by sin can be restored by God's own Son. This is what the apostle Paul speaks about in Ephesians 4:24 and Colossians 3:10. But that is a topic for a later chapter.

MOTHER NATURE?

It is common in many cultures, and also in a number of religions, to speak of the earth as our mother. *Mother Nature* is also an expression that is used frequently. This idea has a long history reaching back to Greek mythology, which referred to the earth as *Gaia*, or *Mother Earth*. Following on the heels of this terminology is the teaching that, as children of the earth, all the citizens of this world must take good care of their aging mother. If they do not, then Mother Earth may become so weak and feeble that she can no longer support and sustain the life of her children. Environmental activists often borrow ideas from the Gaia philosophy.

As stated above, Christians also have a strong motivation for taking the very best care of this earth. However, their motivation is different. It is not because the earth is our aged and increasingly frail mother. Rather, the proper motivation is the confession that the world ultimately belongs not to us but to our heavenly Father, who created it all. In addition, when the Holy Spirit speaks in Scripture about our spiritual mother, he does not point to the earth below but to the Jerusalem above (Gal 4:26; Rev 21:2). This New Jerusalem corresponds to the church (Heb 12:22–23). In fact, John Calvin, one of the reformers of the church in the sixteenth century, said it this way: "To those to whom [God] is a Father, the Church must also be a mother."[1] And it is the church, not the earth, that gives us the gospel, that pure spiritual milk by which we may grow up in our salvation (1 Pet 1:24–2:2).

Suggested Readings: Genesis 1:24–31; 1 Corinthians 11:1–16

QUESTIONS FOR UNDERSTANDING

1. Describe as fully as you can what it means that God created human beings in his own image. Be sure to refer to some relevant Scripture passages.
2. In Psalm 8:5 David speaks about how people were created and he remarks, "You made him a little lower than God and crowned him with glory and honour." (Please note that there are different English translations of this verse, but the original does say "a little lower than *God*"). Read the entire Psalm and discuss how these verses shed light on what it means to be created in God's image.
3. On the basis of the parallel between Genesis 1:26–27 and Genesis 5:1–3, this chapter reaches the conclusion that the image of God has more to do with a Father-children relationship than with the human abilities to think and choose. But do these abilities still form some part of God's image? If so, in what way?
4. Lord's Day 3 of the Heidelberg Catechism identifies three things that flow out of our creation in God's image: man was created

---

1. John Calvin, *Institutes of the Christian Religion*, ed. John T. McNeill (Philadelphia: Westminster Press, 1960), 4.1.1.

"so that [1] he might rightly know God his Creator, [2] heartily love him, [3] and live with him in eternal blessedness to praise and glorify him." In short, then, the threefold purpose of the image of God is to know, to love, and to live with God. How can we grow with respect to each one of these three purposes so that God's image will shine even brighter in us?

QUESTIONS FOR FURTHER DISCUSSION

1. Depression is a condition that affects many people, including Christians. In some situations there are medical factors that require medical treatments. However, often there are also spiritual struggles that complicate the situation. If a fellow Christian is struggling with feelings of worthlessness or lethargy, what kind of spiritual counsel can you provide based on the doctrine of the image of God? What other things can we do or say to help children of God who suffer in this way?

2. Environmental advocates are encouraging everyone to go green and to take better care of the earth, water, plants, and animals. How should Christians evaluate the green movement? Should we promote it? Discourage and avoid it? Or use it carefully and selectively? Please give reasons for your answer.

3. Unbelievers often refer to *Mother Nature* in their conversations. Discuss ways in which the use of that phrase could present you with an opportunity to share the truth of God's Word. How would you approach it? What exactly would you say?

4. In your experience, what kinds of issues or problems arise between men and women, whether they are married or single? If you can, identify *three* such issues and explore how the truth of being equal but not identical before God (i.e., the fact that both genders were made in God's image but also that one was created before the other) might help untangle some of these knots.

CHAPTER 10.

SIN OFFENDS GOD

"Nobody is perfect." Almost everyone has said something like that at some point in his or her life. Have you as well? In fact, people are usually willing to admit—whether sooner or later—that they make mistakes. They may even be willing to describe their mistakes as sins.

Does this mean, though, that we all properly understand our sinfulness? Is it sufficient to admit that we are not perfect? What does someone need to know in order to comprehend the depths of our sinfulness? And why is it so important to know about our sinfulness? After all, isn't this a rather dark and depressing doctrine? We will be exploring these questions in this chapter.

To begin with, we should establish the difference between having guilt feelings according to our conscience and properly understanding our sinfulness according to God's Word. Even people who do not believe in the Lord still feel guilty about certain things. Their conscience accuses them of selfish deeds and foolish desires. The apostle Paul also speaks about this in Romans 2:14–15. There he acknowledges that even though some people have not learned about God's law from Scripture, they still do some of the things required in that law. For example, many unbelievers also honour their parents, which is in accord with the fifth commandment. When this happens, says the apostle Paul, "they show that the work of the law is written on their hearts, while their conscience also bears witness, and their conflicting thoughts accuse or even excuse them" (Rom 2:15).

However, there are problems with guilt feelings generated by our conscience. The first problem is that our conscience is not always reliable. Sometimes it exposes our wrongdoings; other times it overlooks them, or worse yet, it helps us make up excuses for our iniquities. The second, and even bigger, problem with our conscience is that, even when it works properly, it only leaves us with the feeling that we did something wrong. It does not teach us *why* it is wrong. Also, it does not teach us *how wrong* it really is. Therefore, to have a proper understanding of our sinfulness we need something more than our consciences. As the Canons of Dort remind us, the human conscience, which is part of the light of nature, still leaves a person far away from "arriving at the saving knowledge of God and true conversion" (3/4.4).

By contrast the law of God teaches us what the conscience of man cannot divulge to us. The apostle Paul explains, "Yet if it had not been for the law, I would not have known sin" (Rom 7:7). In the first place, the law tells us about *God's* standards for right and wrong, which are far more stringent than our standards. The apostle goes on to comment, "For I would not have known what it is to covet if the law had not said, 'You shall not covet'" (Rom 7:7). Society does not tell you that coveting is wrong. In fact, our consumer society almost makes you feel as if coveting is a civil obligation! However, the law of God says coveting is sin. Second, the law of God makes it clear that when we sin, we are—above all else—offending God. True, sin hurts our neighbour. Yes, by sinning we also wounds ourselves. Yet, beyond that, we need to come to the point of echoing David's words in Psalm 51:4 and saying to the LORD, "Against *you*, you only, have I sinned and done what is evil in your sight." The law of God requires us to confront that uncomfortable reality.

At the same time, when we learn about our sinfulness from God's law, we are also on the path leading to the knowledge of God's saving grace in Christ. "Christ is the end of the law" (Rom 10:4). In other words, if we carefully follow the truth of the law, we should end up at the goal of confessing that Christ, not the law, is our Saviour.

SIN IS A MANY-SIDED MISERY

In Scripture the Holy Spirit uses a number of different words to describe sin. The word *sin* itself (Luke 15:21) has to do with missing the mark. In his law the LORD has set a certain goal or target for our daily living. When we sin, our conduct is like an arrow that misses the target and falls to the ground. In addition to sin, Scripture also speaks of *transgressions* (Mic 7:18) and *trespasses* (Rom 5:15). God's law is not only a goal at which we should aim, but it also provides boundary lines for our desires, words, and actions. However, when we step beyond those God-given boundaries and wander off into the wilds of wickedness, then we are guilty of transgressions or trespasses.

Sin is further described as *disobedience* (Rom 5:19). This term highlights the lack of proper listening that often accompanies sin. Instead of listening, eagerly and obediently, to God's commands, the sinful heart often has selective hearing. It takes what it likes from the Bible and conveniently turns a deaf ear to the rest. When this is left unchecked, disobedience is the kind of attitude that will lead to *rebellion* (Num 14:18). This is another word for sin, which demonstrates that sin is not always a regrettable weakness. Sometimes it is done deliberately and defiantly (Num 15:30), in spite of better knowledge. This is the spirit of rebellion. Rebellion can easily give birth to a spirit of *lawlessness* (2 Thess 2:7). A lawless person is someone who wants to cast off all restraints. He finds the commands of God burdensome and restrictive. To him they are like a straitjacket, and at the first opportunity he wants to rip off the straitjacket and cast it aside. Obviously, the outlook of the lawless one is diametrically opposed to the attitude of the psalmist who sings that the commands of the LORD are "sweeter also than honey and drippings from the honeycomb" (Ps 19:10).

This is only a short survey of the terms that Scripture uses for sin. More words could be mentioned. Yet this should be sufficient to show that sin is much more than just making a mistake, as a student might make an error on his math test. All of us need to come to terms with what this *more* all includes. Our sins have direction; they have a certain evil-seeking tendency to them. They involve wandering off the straight and narrow path with the very real potential that we will stumble again and entangle ourselves in even more iniquity. In addition, our sins are much more than wicked actions. They also demonstrate a wrong attitude. It is an attitude that grates against both the law and the Lawgiver. No one can sin against the law without deeply offending the Lawgiver. When our pride is finally broken and we are willing to say from the heart, "I insulted the Most Holy and Almighty God by my sin," then we are starting to come to grips with the depth of our own depravity.

Moreover, since there are so many deviant aspects to sin, it is not surprising that Jesus Christ had to suffer in so many difficult ways. He was frequently misunderstood, falsely accused, callously betrayed, unjustly condemned, and much more. So, the more we understand and acknowledge the wide extent of our own sinfulness, the more we will realize and value the vast breadth of our Saviour's suffering for our sake.

However, in this analysis of the true depths of sin, we still have to take one more significant step. In order to do so, we need to look at not only the content of sin but also its context. The woman and man who sinned first, Eve and Adam, were created in the image of God. As we learned in the previous chapter, this meant that our first parents were God's first human children. As his children, they also reflected the righteousness and holiness of their heavenly Father. So when Adam and Eve sinned they not only rebelled as creatures against their Creator, or as citizens against their King, but also as children against their own heavenly Father.

As any earthly parent can tell you, nothing pierces your heart quite as much as when your own child intentionally defies your explicit and well-meant instruction. When your own child is rebelling, it is no longer just a rule that is being broken; it is most certainly a relationship that is being marred. In the beginning, God the Father cherished Adam and Eve. He took delight in them, and he saw in them a faithful reflection of his very own perfections, such as his justice and his compassion. But after the fall, that all changed—dramatically. Now, with a paternal heart weighed down with anguish (Gen 6:6), God the Father saw that his own children did not want to listen to him; in fact, they did not even want to meet with him anymore. They would rather run off and hide in the bushes than speak with their own Father (Gen 3:8). They would rather point the finger of guilt at others (Gen 3:12–13) than honestly admit to their Father what they had done wrong. Sin is always horrible, but when it is your own child who deliberately sins against you, that is far worse.

The LORD expresses the pain of his paternal heart in Hosea 11:1–9. There he first recalls all the tender love he has poured into the upbringing of his child, Ephraim, which is another name for the nation of Israel (vv. 1–4). Next, he laments how stubbornly determined his child is to walk away from him (vv. 5–7). Finally, just like an earthly father, so also our heavenly Father cannot simply disown his child. In spite of his child's rebellious attitude, the heavenly Father cannot, and does not, give up on his son (vv. 8–11).

When sin is understood in this way, it can never be merely a moral, or ethical, matter. To be sure, it is that, but it is more. Sin also has a religious quality to it, and that religious aspect has a familial facet, which cannot be ignored. Sin fails to fulfil a moral duty, but it also manages to offend God by showing an appalling degree of dishonour for him and ingratitude for all the loving care that the heavenly Father has lavished upon us (1 John 3:1–3). Thus, once again, when our pride is broken and, like the prodigal son, we are finally willing to own up to our iniquity and say, *"Father*, I have sinned against you" (Luke 15:11–21), then we are truly coming to understand just how awful sin really is.

This familial facet of sin also sheds light on the appearance of God's eternal *Son* as the Saviour. At least theoretically, we might ask, "Why did God the Father give up his own Son for us all?" (Rom 8:32). Why, for instance, did the Father not send the Holy Spirit to suffer and die for our salvation? The straightforward answer is as follows: since it was a son and a daughter who sinned, it was the eternal Son who had to come and save from sin.

INHERITED SIN

The inclination to sin started with Adam and Eve, but it certainly did not end with them. This same sinful nature was found in their children, Cain and Abel. In Cain the sin of jealousy and anger even welled up to the point that he murdered his own brother (Gen 4:8). From Cain, and later Seth, sinfulness was passed down to the next generation, and from them to the generation after them, and so on, right up until the new generation being born today. This transmission of sin from one generation to the next is called *inherited sin* or *original sin*. The Belgic Confession describes it in this way: "It is a corruption of the entire nature of man and a hereditary evil which infects even infants in their mother's womb" (Art 15).

Not surprisingly, this doctrine of original sin has been criticized. For the most part, the criticisms can be grouped into two categories. The first criticism protests that some kind of injustice is being done here. The key question is: why should we suffer today for something that Adam and Eve did thousands of years ago? After all, does not the LORD himself say, "The soul who sins shall die" (Ezek 18:20)? The second criticism focuses on the teaching of the sinfulness of babies, yes, even infants in their mother's womb. This teaching seems to be entirely counter-intuitive. Everyone who has snuggled a newborn in her arms knows this. If there is anyone on earth who is innocent, surely it is an infant. If there is any place on earth that is free from the influence and power of sin, surely it is inside a mother's womb. So, how can the Belgic Confession suggest that sin infects even infants in the womb?

Let us begin with the second criticism. From the start we should admit that the doctrine seems counter-intuitive. To some it may even appear to be completely illogical. However, and this is the key point, it is Scriptural. When our eyes look at a newborn babe, we see innocence. But when the Lord views that same child, he sees what we do not see: the inherited sinful nature that already resides in the heart of that infant. For instance, King David speaks openly about this after he has been found guilty of adultery and murder. In his prayer to God he says, "Behold, I was brought forth in iniquity, and in sin did my mother conceive me" (Ps 51:5). Moreover, Job demonstrates that logic can cut both ways. If there is a sinful father and a sinful mother and together they have a child, why would we expect that the child is suddenly sin-free? Job put it this way: "Who can bring a clean thing out of an unclean? There is not one" (14:4). With a slightly different emphasis, the prophet Jeremiah makes a similar point. He writes, "Can the Ethiopian change his skin or the leopard his spots? Then also you can do good who are accustomed to do evil" (Jer 13:23). Indeed, sin is not only something we learn later on in life; it is also part of our very nature from conception onwards (Eph 2:3). In this way, acknowledging original sin involves a test of our faith: even though little babies do not look sinful, on the basis of God's Word we confess them to be so.

The answer to the first criticism is a bit more involved. The first step is to acknowledge the deep-seated character of sin. As noted above, sin is not merely a mistake; it is also a persistent attitude and a stubborn inclination. This sinful inclination may not immediately manifest itself in all kinds of grievous and evil deeds, but it is still there. A newborn infant does not (yet) hit his older sister or call her nasty names. However, the inclination toward selfishness and jealousy is already there at conception (Ps 51:5), and it is there by way of inheritance.

The second step is to remember that God created Adam and Eve in his image. Therefore at creation it was *like Father, like children.* As God was righteous and holy, so were his first human children. However, then, by their own foolishness, Adam and Eve sinned, thereby exchanging righteousness for unrighteousness, and holiness for uncleanness. Yet, as we know, there was also an image and likeness relationship between Adam and Seth (Gen 5:1–3). Consequently, after the fall, it is also *like father, like child.* Only now the father and spiritual template is Adam, the *sinful* Adam, and the child is Seth. Seth is in the likeness of his earthly father, and since his earthly father is corrupted with sin, he will also mirror that corruption in his own life. This pattern of inheriting the sinfulness of one's parents continues from generation to generation.

On the one hand, the doctrine of inherited sin makes it abundantly clear just how tragic the fall into sin really was. On the other hand, this doctrine also serves as the dark background against which the bright splendour of the incarnation shines. Every baby born into this world has been sinful except one: the baby Jesus. He alone is the Holy One (Luke 1:35), conceived and born without sin (Heb 4:15). His sin-free conception and birth covers over our sinful conception and birth (LD 14). In this way a fuller understanding of sin once more gives us a deeper appreciation for our Saviour.

ACTUAL SIN

Original, or inherited, sin is the inclination toward iniquity that lives inside all of us. Actual sin occurs when that evil inclination becomes a malicious action of the heart, mind, tongue, or body. For example, by nature we are all inclined toward jealousy. However, when a toddler sees that his friend has a toy car he wants, that inclination turns into an actual jealous desire in his heart: he wants to grab that toy, even though it is not his car. Next the sinful desire leads to sinful thoughts. The boy supposes that if he can just wait a moment until his friend has turned his head the other way, he will be able to lay hands on that shiny car. Then the sinful thoughts manifest themselves in sinful actions. The boy implements his plan. He patiently waits, first thirty seconds, then sixty seconds, and yes, no sooner does his friend glance briefly out of the window than he snatches up the toy car and runs away with it. In brief, this is how sin can be dissected. This process is also described by James when he writes, "But each person is tempted when he is lured and enticed by his own desire. Then desire when it has conceived gives birth to sin, and sin when it is fully grown brings forth death" (1:14–15).

Actual sin may be committed against any one of God's commandments, primarily revealed in the Ten Commandments (Exod 20:1–17; Deut 5:6–21). But it is never as simple as sinning against one commandment only. More often than not, sin is a web of wickedness, and many different transgressions stick to that web. To return to the example above, the boy's sin begins as an instance of jealous covetousness, which is a sin against the tenth commandment. That soon leads to snatching away the toy car, a form of stealing, which corresponds to the eighth commandment. In so doing, he is disobeying his parents, who have undoubtedly taught him not to snatch toys away from other children. This disobedience is sin against the fifth commandment. Moreover, even though he may not be aware of it, his jealous, covetous actions also disgrace the LORD whose name he bears and must uphold. This is sin against the third commandment. So, as this small example illustrates, sin has a habit of spiralling from one command to the next, leaving a trail of broken laws behind it. In fact, the apostle James goes so far as to say that "whoever keeps the whole law but fails in one point has become accountable for all of it" (Jas 2:10).

This close unity of the commandments is also emphasized by our Saviour Jesus Christ when he compressed the Ten Commandments into only two: "You shall love the LORD your God with all your heart and with all your soul and with all your mind. This is the great and first commandment. And a second is like it: You shall love your neighbour as yourself" (Matt 22:37–39). In this way "love is the fulfilling of the law" (Rom 13:10). Every sin that can be named involves a lack of love for God, and many sins also involve a lack of love for our neighbor. For this reason the Catechism identifies the core of sin as being an inclination to hatred (LD 2, Q&A 5). Hatred is a strong word, but by the same token sin is an awful reality. To love God is to avoid sin, but to indulge in sin is hatred toward God. Once again, sin is not merely a moral fault; it is a religious offence against the God who made us and maintains us.

The Roman Catholic Church divides actual sins into two categories: venial and mortal. Venial sins are less severe. While they may hinder a person in his spiritual progress, they do not merit everlasting punishment. Mortal sins are more severe. They deprive a person of God's grace and deserve eternal death. For those who commit mortal sins, God's grace can be restored only through the sacraments, especially penance and the mass. Is it right to classify sins according to their severity? In fact, the Saviour from sin, Jesus Christ himself, teaches differently. He said that even one angry outburst such as "you fool!" makes one liable to the fire of hell (Matt 5:22). Thus, sin is not easily pigeonholed into categories of greater or lesser. Rather, we need to recognize that all sin is worthy of being punished by God's curse (Gal 3:10), and it is only through repentance and faith in the crucified Christ that all sins are forgiven (1 John 2:1–2).

TOTAL DEPRAVITY

So far we have learned that sin is a many-sided, inherited iniquity which deeply offends God the Father Almighty. Yet someone might ask, "Is there not still some good in human beings?" After all, your unbelieving neighbour may also help a sick widow living next door by bringing her a meal. Indeed, there are people from many different religions who freely volunteer many hours of their time for good causes. Simply put, Christians do not have a monopoly on charity. So does this not prove that there is a mixture of good and evil in everyone?

Let us first turn to Scripture, the source of all sound theology. In the days of Noah, before the Flood, God surveyed the spiritual landscape of the society of that time. The result was not good. "The LORD saw that the wickedness of man was great in the earth, and that every intention of the thoughts of his heart was only evil continually" (Gen 6:5). This is called total depravity. It refers to the fact that all of a person's faculties—his heart, his mind, his body, and his soul—have been corrupted by sin. For this reason you might even call it pervasive depravity. There is no little, purely holy corner tucked away in the human soul. Total depravity also refers to God's revelation that the totality of the world's population is infected with sin (Rom 3:10). All who are human beings, and all that human beings are, have been contaminated with sin (1 John 1:8).

But what about the unbelievers who help a widow or volunteer at a hospital? It is true that these people do things that are good and right "in natural and civil matters" (CoD 3/4.4). However, this civil righteousness cannot stand before the judgment throne of God and count in any way as spiritual or eternal righteousness. As the Heidelberg Catechism explains, "the righteousness which can stand before God's judgment must be absolutely perfect and in complete agreement with the law of God, whereas even our best works in this life are all imperfect and defiled with sin" (LD 24, Q&A 62). The reason that we are inclined to think that there is a mixture of good and evil in people is that our eyes are not nearly as holy as God's eyes, and our standards of righteousness are far lower than his divine requirements. God is holy, holy, holy, and even after the Flood the LORD still announced that "the intention of man's heart is evil from his youth" (Gen 8:21).

DENYING TOTAL DEPRAVITY AND DIMINISHING CHRIST

Not everyone agrees that human beings are totally depraved. One example is Pelagius, a British-born monk who moved to Rome and lived in and around that area from the end of fourth century on into the beginning of fifth century. Denying the doctrine of original sin, he felt that babies are born into this world with a spiritually clean slate. If later on in life these infants grow up into children who sin, then this sin is something they learned by imitating others rather than by inheriting it from their parents. This false teaching about sin has consequences. Since Pelagius taught that everyone began with a clean slate and everyone has a free will, his constant emphasis was on making the right, godly choices in conduct and speech. While it is certainly laudable to live a holy life, Pelagius set the cross of Christ off in shadows, for in his view man with his free will was already capable of living the holy life, and the work of Christ was needed only to fill in the gaps.

For many, Pelagius was too optimistic about human nature. It is actually hard to deny that something is wrong with human beings already from a very young age. However, instead of confessing total depravity, the Roman Catholic Church as well as others have adopted a watered-down version of Pelagianism, also known as Semi-Pelagianism. This view maintains that instead of being born with a clean slate, human beings are by nature spiritually sick individuals. They need help; they need the medicinal grace provided by Christ in the sacraments. Yet once this help is given, salvation becomes a co-operative effort: human beings do what they can from their side, while God does the necessary remainder in Christ. Neither Pelagianism nor Semi-Pelagianism does justice to the Word of God. Through the apostle Paul, Christ himself teaches that "you were *dead* in the trespasses and sins" (Eph 2:1). This is far different from being born with a clean slate or being spiritually sick. Dead is dead! Those who are spiritually dead need much more than spiritual help and guidance. They need nothing short of a spiritual resurrection. Thankfully, "God, being rich in mercy, because of the great love with which he loved us, even when we were dead in our trespasses, made us alive together with Christ—by grace you have been saved" (Eph 2:4–5).

Suggested Readings: Psalm 51:1–12; Hosea 11:1–9

QUESTIONS FOR UNDERSTANDING

1. List some ways in which you personally tend to diminish the full sinfulness of your sins. Discuss ways in which we can all better grasp the totality of our depravity.
2. What is the light of nature? What can this light do? What can it not do? Canons of Dort 3/4.4 will be helpful.
3. Someone says to you, "I'm sorry, but I just cannot understand how a baby can be sinful even before he can walk or talk." How would you respond? Use Scriptural passages and, if you can, confirm your answer by referring to practical experience.
4. List at least three ways in which a deeper understanding of sin leads to a deeper appreciation of Christ our Saviour. Since a deeper understanding of sin leads to a deeper appreciation of Christ, why do we still have such a strong habit of trying to cover up our sinfulness?

QUESTIONS FOR FURTHER DISCUSSION

1. The Lord Jesus Christ maintains some very strict standards in the Sermon on the Mount. For example, in Matthew 5:28 he says, "But I say to you that everyone who looks at a woman with lustful intent has already committed adultery with her in his heart." At first glance this seems unjust. Is not the actual sin of adultery far more

serious than a few fleeting and lustful thoughts? Why does Jesus Christ preach in this way?

2. Parenting is a challenge. Often dads and moms have to repeat the same warnings over and over again (e.g., "Johnny, how many times have I told you to stop pestering your sister!"). At times parents are also shocked at the disrespect with which their own dear children can treat others. How does the doctrine of original sin help parents come to grips with this? Also, how do we ensure that original sin does not become an excuse for tolerating ungodly behaviour in children?

3. Read Romans 3:9–18. All in all, it is a scathing indictment of how sinful human beings are. Yet the same apostle Paul who wrote those words also said in 1 Corinthians 5:1–2 that pagans sometimes have a higher sense of morality than people in the church. How do we fit these two passages together? In the final analysis, how *total* is total depravity?

4. In James 5:16 we find this exhortation: "Confess your sins to one another and pray for one another, that you may be healed." Do we do this enough? Is it always appropriate to confess our sins to others, or are there times when we should keep it between God and ourselves? And what is the best way to confess sins to each other? To whom? How often? In what level of detail? How do we prevent confession of sin from turning into juicy gossip and ruining reputations?

CHAPTER 11.

COVENANT: GOD'S RELATIONSHIP WITH HIS PEOPLE

The coronation of a new monarch is always marked by ceremony and symbolism. For example, at the coronation of Queen Elizabeth II of the United Kingdom on June 2, 1953, she was given not only a crown but also a royal orb, two different sceptres, and a coronation ring that was placed on the fourth finger of her right hand. Interestingly, this special ring is also called the "Wedding Ring of England." It is a stunning ring glistening with gems of sapphire and ruby.

What does this ring symbolize? And why would it be called the "Wedding Ring of England"? In part, the answer revolves around the key word in this chapter: *covenant*. As we all realize, the queen has an official relationship with, and a solemn responsibility toward, the citizens of her kingdom. According to Scripture this kind of relationship can also be described as a covenant. For example, in the days of Joash the king and Jehoiada the priest, the royal leader and his people were bound together in a covenant agreement (2 Kgs 11:17). In a similar fashion, when a husband and a wife agree to be married, to love and help each other for as long as they both shall live, then the two are united as one in a covenant bond. That is why the prophet Malachi speaks of a wife as joined to her husband "by covenant" (Mal 2:14). So, realizing that both marriage bonds and the relationships between monarchs and their nations can be described as covenants, it is no surprise that the Queen Elizabeth's coronation ring is also called the "Wedding Ring of England."

Right from the start this teaches us a few important things about covenants. First, a covenant relationship is as solemn as it is sacred. Marriage is not a casual agreement; neither is God's relationship with his people. It is special, serious, legally binding, and long-term, indeed lifelong. It is also a delightfully blessed relationship, and that is the second key thing. To be sure, there may be difficult moments, both in marriage and in the relationship between royalty and their nations. However, the LORD has specifically designed a covenant to cultivate and protect a rich, joyful, and deeply meaningful relationship.

Finally, although every covenant involves certain stipulations and ceremonies, let us not forget that, in the end, covenants in the Bible involve personal relationships. In fact, those relationships are the heart and soul of any covenant. For example, in order to be officially married, people need to sign a wedding certificate, but marriage is all about the groom and his bride loving and living together, not just signing a piece of paper. Similarly, a coronation day, with all its pomp and circumstance, is an appropriate event, given the occasion. Yet, what really counts in the long-term is the relationship of mutual loyalty and respect between the ruler and those who are ruled. Bearing this in mind as we look more closely at the details of God's covenant with us, let us always remember: it is not a pragmatic business agreement. Rather, it is a precious, unique marriage relationship (Ezek 16:8).

COVENANT: WHAT IS IT?

The first time that we find the word *covenant* in Scripture is in Genesis 9:9. Paying some attention to the context of this first occurrence is helpful. In short, the LORD had sent the Flood to punish and cleanse the evil society of that time (Gen 6–7). All living creatures, both human and animal, died, except Noah, his family, and the animals they had taken with them in the ark (7:23). However, months later the LORD sent a strong wind, and slowly the floodwaters receded (8:1–5). When all the occupants of the ark finally stepped back onto dry ground, they thanked the LORD with a sacrifice (8:20). The LORD also had some strict instructions for Noah and his family, so that they would not fall back into the sins that originally caused the LORD to send the Flood in the first place. They were to be fruitful and increase in number as well as show respect for each other's lives, steering away from all murderous intentions (9:1, 7).

Needless to say, Noah and his wife, along with his three sons and their wives, must have been more than a little nervous as they made this new beginning in a vast and now mostly unpopulated world. What if they made a mistake? What if they fell back into the old sinful ways? Would there be another flood, and would they be the ones drowning this time? Anxieties such as these must have been swirling around in their thoughts. Therefore, in order to calm their minds and steady their hearts, the LORD makes a covenant with Noah and his children, and indeed, with all living creatures. Here are the LORD'S own words:

> Then God said to Noah and to his sons with him, "Behold, I establish my covenant with you and your offspring after you, and with every living creature that is with you, the birds, the livestock, and every beast of the earth with you, as many as came out of the ark; it is for every beast of the earth. I establish my covenant with you, that never again shall all flesh be cut off by the waters of the flood, and never again shall there be a flood to destroy the earth." And God said, "This is the sign of the covenant that I make between me and you and every living creature that is with you, for all future generations (Gen 9:8–12).

There are a number of noteworthy items here. First of all, God reveals himself here as the God of initiative: "Behold, *I* establish." In fact, so strong is God's initiative that he calls it "*my* covenant." Normally speaking, when a covenant is made between two parties (in this case, God and Noah's family), it would be referred to as *our* covenant. However, here the LORD maintains ownership of the covenant; he calls it "my covenant."

Second, God's covenant immediately includes Noah's descendants. The word used here, *descendants*, refers not only to his own sons—Shem, Ham, and Japheth—but also to any grandchildren and great-grandchildren who would be born in the family over time. In other words, this covenant establishes a relationship that endures through the generations.

Third, this covenant contains a specific promise in which God assures Noah and his descendants that he will never again destroy the earth with a flood. This is exactly the assurance that Noah and his children needed to hear at this particular moment in history, and in his grace and compassion for this family, the LORD provides it. Now they could step forward into this post-Flood era with courage instead of crippling anxiety.

Moreover, should doubts about this promise ever arise in their minds, the fourth element of the covenant would help them, namely, the rainbow, which is the visible sign attached to this covenant. Of course, at times it would still rain very hard, perhaps even to the point of some local flooding, but whenever they saw that rainbow, God was showing them, and us, that no matter what, he would never send another worldwide flood.

Finally, when the LORD makes a promise, he does not go back on his word. He will do as he has promised, and for this reason he describes his covenant as "everlasting" (Gen 9:16). The warranty on God's covenant is not merely a lifetime guarantee; it is an assurance for all time. So, in sum, there are five important aspects in God's covenant with Noah: 1) God's initiative, 2) a relationship that continues through the generations, 3) a specific and gracious promise, 4) a visible sign that confirms the truth of the promise, and 5) an everlasting guarantee.

Later in the book of Genesis, particularly in Genesis 15 and 17, the LORD makes another covenant, this time with Abram. Abram is anxious because he and his wife Sarai have no children (Gen 15:3–4). In this context the LORD comes with assuring words and makes a covenant with him. Remarkably, each of the five above-mentioned elements returns. In the first place, Abram had not asked for a covenant; he had not even mentioned the word. He was yearning for a child, not a covenant. So again, it was entirely the LORD'S initiative to appear to Abram and make a covenant with him (Gen 15:18). A little later, in Genesis 17, when he confirms this covenant with Abram, who is now renamed Abraham, he also indicates that it belongs to him when he calls it "*my* covenant" (Gen 17:2, 4, 7, 9). Second, even though Abraham and Sarah do not have any children of their own yet, the LORD still applies the covenant through the generations. The LORD clearly says that it is "between me and you and your offspring after you throughout their generations for an everlasting covenant, to be God to you and to your offspring after you" (Gen 17:7). Third, this covenant contains two special promises. In due time Abraham would have many descendants (Gen 15:5; 17:6), and the LORD would give the land of Canaan to Abraham's family as their own possession (Gen 15:7; 17:8). Fourth, a sign was attached to this covenant: circumcision (Gen 17:10–14). Fifth, this covenant is also described as being "everlasting" (Gen 17:7, 13). The structural similarities between the covenant with Noah and the one with Abraham are striking, although not entirely surprising. Since the LORD is a God of order and faithfulness, we expect this kind of consistency in his work.

There are still more occasions in Scripture when the LORD makes or confirms a covenant with someone and his family (2 Sam 7, with David and his sons) or with an entire nation (Exod 24, with the Israelites). However, the two examples above give us enough revelation to establish a basic definition of God's covenant. A covenant is *a binding, everlasting relationship between God and his people in which he makes specific gracious promises and gives a visible sign to confirm those promises.* Given the gracious manner in which God established and maintains this covenant, it is often called the covenant of grace. As described earlier, the closest comparison we can make to human agreements is to the marriage covenant (Mal 2:14), a lifelong relationship between a husband and wife, which is often accompanied by a visible sign such as a wedding ring.

COVENANT: HOW DOES IT WORK?

Even though the covenant is initiated by one party, namely God, it obviously involves two parties: God and his people. In the covenant both parties have their own parts to do. This is especially clear in the language of Genesis 17. The LORD says, *"Behold, my covenant . . . ."* (v. 4), and he immediately promises Abraham descendants (vv. 5–6) and land (v. 8). However, then the LORD continues and says to him, *"As for you . . ."* (v. 9), and he gives Abraham the solemn obligation to continue administering the sign, circumcision, without fail from generation to generation (vv. 10–14).

A similar pattern is found in Deuteronomy 28. In this chapter the LORD is renewing his covenant with his people just before they enter the promised land. As for himself, he promises many blessings for his people: children, crops, livestock, security, and much more (vv. 2–12). However, with the LORD'S promises also comes the obligation to obey and serve him alone (vv. 1, 13–14). Furthermore, the LORD warns his people that, if they do not obey him, their disobedience will be punished with a most severe curse (vv. 15–68).

This is the way it works within the covenant. Not only are there two parties involved, there are also two parts, which correspond to the two parties. On the one hand, for his part, the LORD makes his gracious promises. Knowing him, we can always count on him to keep his word. On the other hand, for our part, the LORD lays on us the solemn obligation to live in accordance with his holy will. Failing to fulfil our part of the covenant leaves us under the burden of his curse rather than the bounty of his blessings.

However, this immediately places us in a crisis of the covenant. All of God's people are sinful by inclination and depraved in heart and mind, as we discovered in the previous chapter. Given the reality of inherited sin, undoubtedly disobedience will occur and inevitably the curse will be deserved. In short, the urgent question is this: how can such a sinful people live in a covenant relationship with such a holy God? Surely, this is impossible or, at least, can only end with many curses being heaped upon the heads of God's people! Thankfully, there is an answer to this pressing question. The answer is this: God's covenant contains not only two parties and two parts, but also one mediator.

In the Old Testament the mediator of the covenant was Moses. When the LORD and his people were together at Mount Sinai, the Israelites committed a grave sin. They made a golden calf as an idol (Gen 32:1–4), thereby disobeying the clear command of the LORD (Exod 20:4, 22–23).

The LORD is sufficiently angry with them to wipe out the whole nation and start over with Moses (Exod 32:9–10). Hearing about this, Moses is so angry that he smashes to pieces the tablets with the Ten Commandments, which are also known as the words of the covenant (Exod 34:28). All in all, the covenant seems to be teetering on the brink of obliteration. But just at that moment, Moses steps forward and appeals to the LORD, reminding him of the covenant he made with Abraham, Isaac, and Jacob (Exod 23:13). This mediation is effective. The LORD relents, the people survive, and the covenant still stands.

What began with Moses is fulfilled in Jesus Christ. He is the mediator of the new covenant (Heb 9:15, 12:24). He stands between the Holy Father and his sinful people and, on the basis of the shedding of his blood on the cross, the blood of the new covenant (Luke 22:20), he intercedes for his people. With Christ and his atoning work, the covenant does not merely continue but it grows into a relationship full of abundant blessings (Eph 1:3–14). After all, the LORD designed the covenant to be a relationship in which people would flourish, above all spiritually. However, we should not be deluded: without Christ the covenant would result in curses for all God's people. It is not for nothing that we call it the covenant of *grace*. Thanks be to God for Jesus Christ our Lord and our Mediator (Rom 7:25)!

OLD AND NEW COVENANT

As noted above, God's covenant is everlasting (Gen 17:7). Yet through the prophet Jeremiah the LORD heralds the arrival of a new covenant (Jer 31:31) and "in speaking of a new covenant, he makes the first one obsolete. And what is becoming obsolete and growing old is ready to vanish away" (Heb 8:13). So, how can the covenant be everlasting and yet obsolete at the same time?

In order to answer that question, we need to identify precisely what prompted the LORD to make this transition from the old to the new covenant. As the LORD declares in Jeremiah 31, a new covenant was necessary because his people broke his covenant even though he was a husband to them (v. 32). In other words, the problem was not with the covenant itself. The covenant was a good arrangement; in fact, it was a splendidly gracious relationship. The problem, though, was with the people with whom the LORD had made this covenant. Even though God was patient, compassionate, and loving toward them—more than the finest earthly husband ever was toward his wife—his people rebelled, repeatedly running off to worship idols. In reality God's bride, the people of Israel, was a serial adulteress, repeatedly breaking the marriage covenant with her heavenly Husband.

Added to this was the fact that the sacrifices for sin in the old covenant were not truly effective in removing the sin. It is "impossible for the blood of bulls and goats to take away sins" (Heb 10:4), and, therefore, all those animals sacrifices only amounted to "a reminder of sins every year" (Heb 10:3). So, in short, the situation was as follows: a stubbornly sinful and spiritually adulterous nation was living in a binding covenant relationship with a holy God on the basis of sacrifices that could not truly take away even one single sin. Surely, such a situation is unsustainable! Yes, and this is why God, in his good time, made the transition from the old to the new covenant. It was not because the old covenant was a mistake that needed to be corrected. Rather, it was because sinful people need substantial and lasting forgiveness, not merely a shadowy and temporary pardon (Col 2:17; Heb 10:1, 16–18).

This also means that moving from the old to the new is a transition of shadow to substance, of promise to fulfilment. It is *not* a transition from one kind of relationship to a fundamentally different kind of arrangement. The basic structure of the old covenant is continued in the new. Both old and new belong to the same covenant of grace. It simply becomes "a better covenant" (Heb 7:22; 8:6). The five characteristics of the covenant, mentioned earlier, return in the new covenant. It is still initiated by God ("I will make a new covenant," Jer 31:31), continued through the generations, ("the promise is for you and for your children," Acts 2:39), filled with even more gracious promises ("enacted on better promises," Heb 8:6), confirmed by a visible sign ("having been buried with him in baptism," Col 2:11–12), and guaranteed forever ("it is impossible for God to lie," Heb 6:13–20). In this way the everlasting covenant of Genesis 17:7 is also the new covenant of Jeremiah 31:31. The new is not radically different, but it is substantially better. Since the new fulfils the old, the everlasting nature of the old covenant is simply absorbed by, and confirmed in, the new.

At this juncture we should note the view of the *dispensationalists*, those who teach that there is a more radical difference between the old and the new covenants. There are different varieties of dispensationalists, but the vast majority of them teach that while the old covenant carried on through the generations, the new covenant is made only with the elect, not with believing parents and their descendants after them. Close attention to the wording of Scripture proves, however, that dispensationalism is incorrect. In Genesis 17:7 God says to Abraham, "I will establish my covenant between me and *you and your offspring* after you." These words are almost identical to Acts 2:39, where God makes the promises of forgiveness and the Holy Spirit "for *you and your children*." The similarity is too great to be merely a coincidence, especially since the same Holy Spirit inspired both passages.

Moreover, in 1 Corinthians 7:14 the apostle Paul specifically states that the children of believing parents are holy, that is, separated from the world and included among God's people. Added to that, the words of the Lord Jesus Christ himself are significant: "Do not think that I have come to abolish the Law or the Prophets; I have not come to abolish them but to fulfil them" (Matt 5:17). When we pull all these passages together, it should be clear that both covenants, the old and new, continue from generation to generation.

WAS THERE A COVENANT IN PARADISE?

There is an interesting verse in the prophecy of Hosea: "Like Adam they transgressed the covenant; there they dealt faithlessly with me" (6:7). This verse seems to suggest that just as the Israelites were in covenant with the LORD (see Exod 24:8), so was Adam, and that both parties broke their respective covenants. But the curious thing is that when we turn to the account of Adam and Eve in Gen 1–3, we do not read anything about a covenant. Certainly, the word *covenant* does not appear in the first three chapters of the Bible. Therefore some theologians look for elements or aspects of the covenant in those chapters. They identify the command to stay away from the tree of the knowledge of good and evil as the obligation of the covenant (Gen 2:17). They point to the implied gift of eternal life as the promise of the covenant (Gen 2:17). Some even suggest that the two special trees—the tree of the knowledge of good and evil and the tree of life (Gen 2:9)—were signs of the covenant. This covenant in Paradise is mentioned in the Westminster Confession, where it is called the *covenant of works* (Ch 7.2), and in the Westminster Shorter Catechism, which refers to it as the *covenant of life* (Q&A 12). In the course of history, other names have been given to this covenant, such as covenant at creation, covenant of favour, and covenant of love.

This discussion is an example of a matter in which Christians may hold slightly different opinions without accusing each other of false teaching. It is true that the term *covenant of works*, although well known, can be misleading. It might leave the impression that in the Garden, Adam had to merit or earn eternal life. However, even before the fall, whatever Adam received, he received as a gift from God. God does not owe us anything, whether inside or outside of Paradise. At the same time, using terms like *covenant of works* and covenant of grace helps to highlight the fact that something fundamental changed with the fall into sin. After Adam and Eve ate from the forbidden tree, it was most certainly not business as usual within the covenant. As explained earlier in this chapter, sinful people and a holy God can co-exist in covenant relationship only if God graciously provides a mediator, Jesus Christ, in whom people must believe for their salvation (Acts 4:12). Thus, the term *covenant of grace* applies. It was for the same reason—that is, for highlighting the difference between the pre- and post-fall situations—that others have distinguished between the *covenant of favour* in Paradise and the *covenant of grace* after sin entered the world. Rather than insist that one particular term or another must be used, it is more important to understand what people mean by these terms and to ensure that the way they use them lines up with what Scripture teaches.

Beyond discussing the pros and cons of various terms related to the covenant, it is helpful to step back and remind ourselves of what we do know, clearly and confidently. The relationship between God and Adam and Eve is clearly established in Genesis 1:26–27 when human beings were created in the God's image. In chapter 9, we discovered that by looking at Genesis 1:26–27 along with 5:1–3, it becomes evident that the image of God speaks of a Father-children relationship.

Now the relationship between Father and children does have some covenant-like qualities to it. First, like a covenant, the Father-children relationship is not a temporary, fleeting arrangement. Once a father, always a father. Once a son or daughter, always a son or daughter. Both the covenant and the image of God have a certain enduring permanence about them. Second, in the bond between Father and children, the Father makes promises, and the children have an obligation to honour him. Third, as the covenant continues through the generations, so does the image of God (Gen 5:1–3). It is also true, however, that the image of God is not the same thing as the covenant. A special ceremony or sign, such as circumcision (Gen 17:11) or sprinkling of blood (Exod 24:6–8), accompanies a covenant, but there is no comparable symbol for the image of God.

Perhaps we can best sum it up in this way. Being created in God's image established a Father-children relationship between God and Adam and Eve. Like all Father-children relationships, this bond was permanent, and since there was no sin yet, it was a bond completely full of bliss. Since they were God's children, Adam and Eve had an obligation to obey their Father's commands. Again, since there was no sin yet, this obligation was a pure delight to them. Fulfilling this obligation did not merit or earn anything, but it did honour the Father, and that, after all, is the goal of being created in God's image.

Tragically, Adam and Eve disobeyed their Father. The image was corrupted; the relationship was broken. Yet, thankfully, God the Father graciously took the initiative to restore what his children had destroyed. God uses the bond of the everlasting covenant of grace to begin this restoration work. Through the covenant, God's chosen people are brought back into close communion with him. Through the covenant, the blessings of forgiveness and eternal life are extended to them. Through the covenant, sinful people even receive the blessing of being adopted as God's children (Rom 9:4, "to them belong the adoption [and] the covenants"). In short, through the covenant, in Jesus Christ, and by the power of the Holy Spirit, God restores what Adam and Eve forfeited in Paradise. Miraculously, stubborn sinners can once again be called "children of God, and if children, then heirs—heirs of God and fellow heirs with Christ" (Rom 8:16–17). You might even say that in the marriage covenant between Christ and his church (Eph 5:32) we are born anew by the Holy Spirit (John 3:5), according to the image and likeness of God's eternal Son (Rom 8:29), to be the Father's dear children and heirs, who will one day receive the new creation as our own—most certainly unmerited—inheritance (Rev 21:5, 7).

Suggested Readings: Genesis 17:1–14; Hebrews 8:1–7

QUESTIONS FOR UNDERSTANDING

1. The fact that God always takes the initiative in redeeming his people says something about his nature or his perfections. Look back at the list of God's perfections in chapter 5 and identify which ones shine forth most brightly in the initiatives that God takes in Genesis 3, 6, and 12.

2. The LORD also made a covenant with David (2 Chron 21:7). This covenant is described in detail in 2 Samuel 7:1–17. Of the five characteristics of a covenant identified in this chapter, how many can you find in this covenant with David? Briefly describe each element that you find.

3. Identify the two parts of every covenant. What happens if God's people do not keep their part of the covenant? Some passages speak of God's people breaking the covenant (e.g., Lev 26:15; Deut 31:16; Ezek 16:59). Yet, at the same time, the covenant is everlasting (Gen 17:7; Heb 13:20). So, how do those two fit

together? How can an everlasting covenant be broken, yet still exist?

4. List two things that remained the same within the covenant in the transition from old to new. Then list two things that changed. How do we give full recognition to the significant progress that God has made in moving from old to new without slipping into the error of dispensationalism?

QUESTIONS FOR FURTHER DISCUSSION

1. Read Ezekiel 16. In verses 1–58 the LORD tells something like a parable in which he describes finding an abandoned girl whom he eventually marries (v. 8). Sadly, she is unfaithful to him and runs off after other lovers. At the end of the chapter, in verses 59–63 the LORD goes on to apply this to his covenant relationship with his people. List and discuss three things that you, after having meditated on this chapter, appreciate more about being part of God's covenant of grace.

2. The new covenant, as well as the old, includes the children of believers. What comfort does this give to parents? Refer to Canons of Dort 1.17. What responsibilities does this bring to parents? On the one hand, when the privileges of the covenant are emphasized, it sometimes happens that covenant children develop a false sense of security and assume that they will be blessed no matter how they live, even if they indulge in an ungodly lifestyle. On the other hand, when the need for holy living is stressed, covenant children are sometimes led into doubt, or even despair, about their salvation. How do parents find the right balance? Give practical suggestions, if possible.

3. We often speak about God's covenant with believers and their children. But what about God's covenant with "every living creature" (Gen 9:10) and "with day and night and the fixed order of heaven and earth" (Jer 33:25)? What are the implications of this covenant? What assurance does it provide? Discuss how the following three things are related to, or opposed to, each other:

God's covenant with creation, stewardship, and the green movement (ecology).

4. Do you think the relationship in Paradise between God and his first two children, Adam and Eve, is best described as a covenant relationship? If so, what is the best term to describe it: covenant at creation, covenant of works, covenant of life, covenant of favour, or covenant of love? Or do you have a better suggestion of your own?

CHAPTER 12.

ELECTION: GOD'S DECISION TO ADOPT

Laura did not grow up in a Christian home. However, she did live next to a Christian family, the Wilsons. Much to Laura's delight, the Wilsons had a girl that was exactly the same age as she was. Her name was Jane. Laura and Jane spent a lot of time together, dressing up dolls and building play forts. Whenever Laura had a meal at Jane's place, something happened that was new to her: the Wilsons read from the Bible, prayed, and even sang a song about God together. Even though it was unfamiliar to her, Laura liked it, especially when she learned some of the songs and could sing along.

As the girls grew up together, Laura started to ask Jane some questions. Where does God live? What is he like? Who is Jesus? And why do you pray so often for your sins to be forgiven? Jane did her best to answer, and Jane's Mom helped out when her friend's questions became too hard. For a few summers Laura also came to the Vacation Bible School at Jane's church. She enjoyed it, and it generated even more questions in her mind. On some Sundays she would also go to church with Jane's family. She did not comprehend everything the minister said, but she could follow the main lines, and it encouraged her. At a minimum she understood that believing in the death and resurrection of Jesus Christ made things right between God and sinners, including herself, and she liked the idea that all would be well between God and her.

Laura's parents were not opposed to her interest in the Christian faith, but they did not encourage it either. As Laura's Dad always said, "Religion is a matter of personal choice. People have to make up their own minds about whether they want to be religious or not. And the same goes for you, Laura." Well, years later, when she was sixteen, Laura did make up her own mind. She announced to her parents that she wanted to join Jane's church. True to his word, Laura's Dad responded, "That's OK, my girl; you're old enough to make up your own mind about religion. And the Wilsons are a nice family. Just don't expect your mother and me to come along with you." Inwardly Laura was saddened that her parents showed no interest in "religion," as her Dad called it, but she was glad they did not stop her from joining Jane's church.

Joining Jane's church meant learning more about the Bible from Jane's pastor. Once a week Laura, as well as an interested couple, sat down with the pastor and learned all kinds of things about what God teaches in Holy Scripture. One evening they were introduced to something Jane had never heard of before. It was called *election*, or sometimes *predestination*. It was not an easy lesson, but the big picture was clear enough. The pastor said that even before the world and human beings were created, God had already chosen the people whom he wanted to save and adopt as his own children in Jesus Christ.

Curious as always, Laura had her questions about election. She asked the pastor, "If God decided to save me before the creation of the world, how come it does not feel like it happened that way? I was the one who decided to become a Christian. I remember it very well. I prayed about it, even though I was not quite sure how to pray or what words to use. But I prayed anyway. And I kept going back and forth in my mind. Finally, one day I decided that I would do it. I told my parents. And Jane helped me get into your New to the Reformed Faith class. So why does the Bible say that God decided, when I feel like I decided?" That's a good question. And Laura had another one as well. She also asked, "If God decided to save some people before he even created any human beings, doesn't that turn us more or less into robots? God programs us either for salvation or for condemnation. And, in the end, all we're doing is acting out what God has programmed us to do. Does God really want to turn us into robots?" That is also a good question.

Especially considering Laura's personal, spiritual journey, you can understand the questions that she had. In fact, the doctrine of election disquiets people in other ways too. They may be concerned that teaching about predestination will inevitably lead to lazy and careless Christians. After all, if an elect person is assured of his eternal salvation, why not go ahead and live today as the sinful heart desires? Election would appear to undermine the incentive for resisting temptation and striving after holiness.

Another common and perhaps more forceful objection to the doctrine of election is that it just does not seem fair. If even before the creation of the world God had already chosen some unto eternal salvation, while decreeing that others would be eternally condemned, then the reprobate, as the non-elect are called, never even have a chance. At least, that is the impression that people have. Before they could consciously make an informed decision, before they even had a chance to listen to the gospel, indeed, before they took their first breath of air, the fate of the reprobate was already sealed by God's decree. Somehow that just does not seem fair. But as we hope to see in this chapter, these questions, concerns, and objections begin to fade away if we pay close attention to what the God himself says about this doctrine.

ELECTION IS IN THE BIBLE

It is perfectly understandable that people have questions about the doctrine of election. However, all the questions in the world will not change the fact that this teaching is found in the Bible, and that is where we must begin.

Three well-known passages clearly demonstrate that it is biblical to believe in election. The first is Romans 8:29–30: "For those whom [God] foreknew he also predestined to be conformed to the image of his Son, in order that he might be the firstborn among many brothers. And those whom he predestined he also called, and those whom he called he also justified, and those whom he justified he also glorified." God foreknew, or knew ahead of time, those whom he had predestined to final glory. He also planned what was necessary to bring them to that glory, such as their calling and their justification.

The second passage is Ephesians 1:4–5: "He chose us in [Christ] before the foundation of the world, that we should be holy and blameless before him. In love he predestined us for adoption as sons through Jesus Christ, according to the purpose of his will." This passage teaches that God's choice took place before the creation of the world. It also reveals that the basis of election is found in God, in *his* pleasure and will.

This same truth is confirmed in a third passage, 2 Timothy 1:9–10. There we read that God "saved us and called us to a holy calling, not because of our works but because of his own purpose and grace, which he gave us in Christ Jesus before the ages began." Especially that last phrase underlines that God's gracious plan of salvation was not an afterthought, formed in God's mind subsequent to the fall into sin. Rather it was securely there, in a divine decree, even before the beginning of time.

Considered together, these three passages make it quite clear that already in eternity God had a plan in which he made a sovereign choice to pluck some sinners from the punishment into which they would plunge themselves and, instead, to bless them as his own children. This revealed truth also fits with God's perfections and his name (see chapter 5). Since he is the almighty, eternal, and wise God, we would expect that he has a clear and comprehensive plan for all things, which we commonly call providence. But then we would also, and even especially, expect that he would have a clear plan for his central work of salvation. This is what we commonly call election. Furthermore, since God is the great I AM WHO I AM, we are not surprised to hear that just as he planned salvation before the creation of the world, so he will also bring that plan to fruition in final glory. I AM WHO I AM is the God of consistency. He does what he decrees.

So, if election is revealed in Scripture and it fits with God's name and perfections, we have every reason to affirm it in faith. Still, we have to be sensitive to the questions and objections that can arise concerning this doctrine. How do we do so?

BE QUICK TO LISTEN, SLOW TO SPEAK

The title of this section is taken from James 1:19. There the apostle writes, "Know this, my beloved brothers: let every person be quick to hear, slow to speak, slow to anger." Of course, in the first place this text instructs us about how we speak to, or about, other people. At the same time, what applies in our communication with each other, also applies in a certain way to doing theology. Sometimes we hear about a certain teaching, such as election, and we are quick to voice all kinds of questions and objections. However, have we first listened to the Lord? Do we rightly understand what election is, where and how it is revealed, and why God teaches us about it? Truth be told, we are often guilty of being quick to speak and slow to listen, also in theology. However, our goal is to turn that around and listen to the Lord first.

If we start at the beginning, in Genesis 1, it is striking that the Lord does not say anything about the doctrine of election. Many details concerning his creative work are given, but there is not even one word regarding predestination. Logically and chronologically, Genesis 1 seems to be an entirely appropriate place for the Lord to begin speaking about predestination. After all, God made this decree "before the foundation of the world" (Eph 1:4). Therefore, theoretically, the LORD could have included a few verses, or even a chapter, prior to Genesis 1:1, outlining the basic contents of his eternal decree, including both election and reprobation. Remarkably, though, there is no Genesis 0. The starting point of God's revelation is, most clearly, creation, not election.

After speaking about creation in Genesis 1–2, the LORD teaches us about the fall into sin and its immediate consequences in Genesis 3–5. Still, in these chapters there is nothing about election. This same pattern continues in Genesis 6–17. We learn about the Flood, God's covenant with Noah and his family, and the covenant the LORD made with Abraham and his descendants (Gen 15, 17). In fact, it is not until Genesis 18:19 that we hear the first hint of God's ways in election. There the LORD says concerning Abraham, "For I have chosen him, that he may command his children and his household after him to keep the way of the LORD by doing righteousness and justice."

Still, Genesis 18:19 is not much more than a hint about election. Actually, it is not until the book of Deuteronomy that some significant details concerning God's choosing are revealed. In Deuteronomy 7:7, 8 we learn the following from Moses:

> It was not because you were more in number than any other people that the LORD set his love on you and chose you, for you were the fewest of all peoples, but it is because the LORD loves you and is keeping the oath that he swore to your fathers, that the LORD has brought you out with a mighty hand and redeemed you from the house of slavery, from the hand of Pharaoh king of Egypt.

These verses reveal that the basis for the LORD'S choice of his people did not lie in the people themselves—not in how numerous they were, let alone how good they were (Deut 6:17). Rather, he chose them because of what lies within himself: his loyal love. However, even this revelation is limited, for it is about God's choice to redeem the Israelites out of their earthly misery as slaves in Egypt. Strictly speaking, the LORD is not yet teaching us about election unto eternal salvation. He is speaking about choosing a certain group of people to be his covenant people. The revelation of God's eternal decree unto final salvation does not strongly come to the fore until the New Testament. Jesus Christ speaks of God's elect who will be spared on the final day of judgment (Mark 13:20, 27). The apostle Paul, though, is the one who deals with this doctrine most elaborately, writing such key passages as Romans 8–11 and Ephesians 1.

Clearly, the LORD does not avoid this doctrine, but he does purposefully delay his revelation of it. We learn about creation, the fall into sin, and the beginning work of redemption, and then—only then—do we slowly begin to hear about the God who elects. As the Most Wise Teacher, the LORD our God not only knows what we should learn; he also knows the order in which we should learn it. There is definite progress in divine revelation. It is true, chronologically speaking, that election precedes creation and the fall into sin. However, pedagogically speaking, we should begin with creation and the fall and then include election as part of God's saving work. Also, since the LORD teaches us about his covenant (Gen 6, 15, 17) before election, we should be careful that we do not let election dominate our understanding of the covenant, but rather understand election within the context of the covenant. (If you are eager for more on this particular topic, note that we will look at election and covenant in detail at the end of this chapter.)

The Belgic Confession is careful to follow this order. The doctrine of creation and providence is confessed in Articles 12–14. The truth of our fall into sin is dealt with in Articles 14–15. Then, in Articles 16–17, we learn about election in connection with the rescue of fallen man. Likewise, the Canons of Dort are also diligent about speaking about election after confessing the fall into sin. It is noteworthy that each of the five chapters of the Canons of Dort starts with some aspect of our sinfulness (CoD 1.1; 2.1; 3/4.1–5; 5.1–2, 4–5). Following this confessional and wise approach, this book is structured in a similar way. The doctrines of creation and providence (chapters 7–9), sin (chapter 10), and covenant (chapter 11) all precede this present chapter concerning God's election.

Why is this important? In short, if we make election the starting point of our thinking and our theology, we will inevitably run into some of the problems and objections that were mentioned in the introduction. To give one example, if you immediately begin by thinking that God chose some to be saved and others to be condemned, then it will not be long before your mind begins to protest: that's not fair; why some and not others? However, now let us follow the order in which God teaches us. First, we work through the doctrine of creation and stand in awe of how wisely and perfectly God made everything. Next, we take time to acknowledge just how deeply offensive our sins are to God. At this point, we must confess that if we want to speak about what is fair, then it would be just and fair if God condemned each and every person in the whole world to suffer eternal punishment (CoD 1.1). If God would elect only one person unto eternal salvation, that would already be far more than he was ever obliged to do. Yet since the LORD has chosen "many" (Matt 8:11), not just one or two, we have all the more reason to praise God's overflowing grace and avoid any protest that accuses him of being unfair. Evidently, the order of learning doctrine does make a difference, and it can at least begin to settle a disquieted soul.

Another part of being quick to listen and slow to speak is paying careful attention to the way in which the apostle Paul links predestination and adoption. This is found in Ephesians 1:4–5. Here, once again, are those verses: "He chose us in him before the foundation of the world, that we should be holy and blameless before him. In love he *predestined* us for *adoption* as sons through Jesus Christ, according to the purpose of his will." Often when people think of God's election, they imagine that in his mind's eye God foresaw the whole mass of humanity standing before him as an enormous and innocent crowd of people. Then, so they think, the Sovereign One arbitrarily picked a person here and a person there, sending some on the path to heaven while directing others down the road to hell. That is *not* the picture revealed in Ephesians 1. Instead of an innocent crowd, we need to think of orphaned children. Only, these orphans are not nice, sweet, pitiable children. Instead, by nature they are filled with hatred and bitterness; they are bent on living immoral lifestyles (Eph 2:1–3; LD 2, Q&A 5). They are spiritual orphans, not because their parents died, but because they have rebelled and run away from the household of God.

Yet, here is the wonder of God's electing grace: already in eternity the heavenly Father took a decision to adopt some of these rebels, these runaway sinners, and make them his own children. Please note that election is God's decision to adopt, not to take some sinners in as foster children. Foster children receive a clean bed, some warm food, and loving care, but adopted children receive all of that and so much more, including an eternal inheritance. Obviously, when God the Father's election is understood in terms of adoption, it is filled with divine warmth, love, and generosity. This is far different from the other, incorrect picture of a stern, cold Ruler who callously sends people in one eternal direction or another.

FOCUSING ON SOME DETAILS

Undoubtedly, the doctrine of election is a challenging teaching. However, the first chapter of the Canons of Dort helps us out by providing a summary of the whole doctrine in one sentence. It is a long sentence, but here it is:

> Election is the unchangeable purpose of God whereby, before the foundation of the world, out of the whole human race, which had fallen by its own fault out of its original integrity into sin and perdition, he has, according to the sovereign good pleasure of his will, out of mere grace, chosen in Christ to salvation a definite number of specific persons, neither better nor more worthy than others, but involved together with them in a common misery (CoD 1.7).

Let us look at this summary detail by detail. First of all, election is *the unchangeable purpose of God*. As mentioned earlier, this has everything to do with God's name and his perfections. The LORD is not a capricious God who acts in a spontaneously haphazard way. On the contrary, he plans carefully and wisely, and then he executes that plan in a sovereign and steady fashion. Psalm 33:11 celebrates that truth in these words: "The counsel of the LORD stands forever, the plans of his heart to all generations."

Second, election occurred *before the foundation of the world*. This fact, revealed both in Ephesians 1:4 and 1 Peter 1:20, might cause people to wonder why God would choose people who did not even exist yet. We are not able to answer this question fully. After all, the LORD'S thoughts are far higher than our thoughts (Isa 55:9). However, on the one hand, this truth clearly reveals God's eternity. He created time and is sovereign over it; we dwell in time and are subject to it. Therefore, what is perplexing to us is perfectly sensible to him. On the other hand, this truth also reminds us in an unmistakable way that our salvation is not a cooperative effort between God and us, but only and entirely a work of God's grace. Obviously, we were not there when God elected us before the creation of the world. Our parents and grandparents were not there either. Even our first parents, Adam and Eve, had not yet been created. So how could we, or any of our ancestors, have made even the slightest contribution toward our salvation? Obviously, those who do not exist cannot assist.

Third, God's election is *out of the whole human race*, but notice especially that the Canons of Dort go on to further describe this human race as having *fallen by its own fault out of its original integrity into sin and perdition*. Here again you see how this confession carefully follows the order in which God reveals things in his Word. Romans 8:28–30 is the classic passage concerning predestination. Yet these verses immediately follow a passage about suffering, groaning, and weakness—all of which are a result of the fall into sin (Rom 8:18–27). Thus, as a summary of what Scripture teaches, the Canons of Dort are justified in describing election as God's choice out of the fallen human race. Even though, chronologically speaking, election happened before the fall, election is, scripturally speaking, revealed after the fall.

Fourth, the Canons specify that God elected *according to the sovereign good pleasure of his will, out of mere grace*. This emphasis is important because the choices that *we* make are often motivated by something in the object that is chosen. Why does someone choose a Honda rather than a Toyota when buying a car? Likely there is something about the features, the styling, or the price of the Honda that catches the eye of the purchaser. However, what is true of human choice is not true of this divine choice. The reason for God's choice lies entirely within himself, not at all in the people chosen. The Canons underline this at the end of the sentence quoted above when they add that the elect are *neither better nor more worthy than others, but involved together in a common misery*. The apostle Paul confirms this in 2 Timothy 1:9 when he says that God "saved us and called us to a holy calling, not because of our works but because of his own purpose and grace, which he gave us in Christ Jesus before the ages began."

Fifth, God's decision to save his elect people was made *in Christ*. Thus, the Father's choice was not arbitrarily made but rather centred on Christ.

That makes a big difference. The redemptive work of Christ—his incarnation, death, resurrection, and ascension—is the axis around which all of world history revolves. Surely, this axis was not set in place by chance, but "according to the definite plan and foreknowledge of God" (Acts 2:23). Just as surely, this axis was not set in place in vain, but rather to save his people from their sins (Matt 1:21). So, since the Son was foreordained to be the Saviour, the Father also foreordained which people were to be saved. After all, what is a Saviour if he has no people to save? Therefore, from eternity, the Father gave the chosen ones to his Son and, in due time, the Son gave eternal life to them (John 17:2, 6–7).

Finally, God has chosen *a definite number of specific persons*. This means that God's choice was not vague or general. God did not simply decide that he would save *a* people but then fail to specify which particular persons would be included in that people. Such an approach would not fit with God's perfections. God's omniscience teaches us that he knows both the big picture and the particular details. If God knew that he wanted to save a people but did not know the particular persons he wanted to save, then he would not know everything. Thankfully, though, our God does know everything (Heb 4:13), including the exact number of people whom he has chosen to be saved.

These further details on election help us to answer some of the questions that arise concerning this doctrine. Since election is God the Father's gracious decision to save sinners by giving up his own beloved and eternal Son Jesus Christ to die on the cross, how can we still accuse *this* God of being unfair? Added to that, who could ever remain spiritually slothful when so much gratitude is owed to such a gracious God? And, if even our spiritual biography includes a day on which we decided to serve the LORD (Josh 24:15), is it not obvious that God's eternal choice, made before we even existed, takes precedence? Moreover, the only reason that we want to serve him is that he decided beforehand to work that desire in us (Phil 2:13). Finally, as Ephesians 1:4–5 demonstrates, God's election does not turn humans into robots; rather, it turns sinful rebels into adopted children. In short, the more fully we understand the doctrine of election, the more noticeably the objections fade away.

BACK TO THE BASIS: WHY DID GOD ELECT?

Important in this connection is Jacob Arminius, a Dutch theologian who lived from 1559 until 1609. Arminius was concerned about some theologians who presented the doctrine of election in such a way that it almost made God sound like a cold and capricious dictator who arbitrarily spared some and callously condemned others. Therefore, although he did not want to reject predestination entirely, he came up with another way to explain it. He taught that before the creation of the world, God looked ahead in time and took note of those people who, once the earth was created and they were alive, would believe in him. Using this foreknowledge, so Arminius argued, God decided, before creation, to save for all eternity those who would believe in him. This teaching is commonly called *election on the basis of foreseen faith* (CoD 1.9).

The main error in this teaching is that ultimately it places the reason for God's choice in human beings rather than in God himself. In Ephesians 1 the apostle Paul emphasizes that God's election and salvation are "according to the purpose of *his* will" (v. 5), "according to the riches of *his* grace" (v. 7), "according to *his* purpose" (v. 9), and "according to the purpose of *him* who works according to the counsel of *his* will" (v. 11). The point is obvious: the basis of God's election is found in him, not in us. In addition to contradicting Scripture, the Arminian view of election also undermines our assurance of salvation (CoD 1.12–13). Indisputably, all of us are more fickle than we care to admit. Spiritually we have high peaks and low valleys. We change our minds and lose our direction. Therefore, if our election depended, even a little, on ourselves, then we could never be certain of our salvation. Thankfully, our election is based entirely on God's good pleasure and grace. So, looking in faith to him alone, we can be sure of what we hope for and certain of what we do not yet see (Heb 11:1).

REPROBATION

Reprobation is the other side of God's eternal decree. The Bible, as the book of good news, says far more about election than reprobation. However, the Lord does tells us that he not only chose to show compassion to some; he also decided to harden others. As the apostle Paul writes, "So then he has mercy on whomever he wills, and he hardens whomever he wills" (Rom 9:18). It is noteworthy that the apostle puts forward Pharaoh as an example of how God hardens someone (Rom 9:17). Several times in the book of Exodus we hear that Pharaoh and his officials hardened themselves (Exod 8:15, 32; 9:34). Yet we also learn that God hardened Pharaoh's heart (Exod 7:3; 9:12; 10:20; 14:8). Here we stand before a mystery that we cannot fully fathom, and we must be careful not to curiously inquire beyond what our mental capacities allow (BC 13).

Nevertheless, two things need to be mentioned. In the first place, Pharaoh, and anyone else who hardens his heart against God, is accountable for that sin. They cannot blame God for their own rebellion (Jas 1:13–15). Beyond this, we should remember that fallen human beings are inclined by nature to hate God and their neighbours (LD 2). They are neither innocent nor neutral. If God chooses to leave them in their rebellion, then he has done nothing wrong. If he decides to turn them away from the path of destruction on which they have set themselves and grant them eternal life instead, then he has done something very gracious.

Second, God sometimes chooses to harden people in their sins in order to display the brightness of his compassion against the dark background of their stubbornness. As the apostle Paul explains:

> What if God, desiring to show his wrath and to make known his power, has endured with much patience vessels of wrath prepared for destruction, in order to make known the riches of his glory for vessels of mercy, which he has prepared beforehand for glory—even us whom he has called, not from the Jews only but also from the Gentiles? (Rom 9:22–24)

In other words, we, who are nothing but clay, should not presume to criticize the divine Potter concerning the manner in which he shapes the various clay jars on the spinning wheel of his sovereignty. "Will what is moulded say to its moulder, 'Why have you made me like this?' Has the potter no right over the clay, to make out of the same lump one vessel for honourable use and another for dishonourable use?" (Rom 9:20–21)

The answer to this question is most certainly yes; the Potter has the right to shape his clay according to his plan and desire.

Before leaving this topic of reprobation, we should still say a word about God's children who sometimes fear that they have been left out of God's electing grace. In short, they are afraid that they might be reprobate. In the first place, if you have had such fears, or if you know someone who worries about this, be assured that you are not alone. The Canons of Dort even dedicate a whole article to this topic: Chapter 1, Article 16. Obviously, the authors of this confession knew how often such anxieties can arise. The response of the confession is tenderly pastoral. Sometimes there are those who believe in the Lord but whose faith is so weak that they worry if they are perhaps reprobate. Then, there are also those Christians who fall into serious sins or who just cannot seem to resist temptation as consistently and effectively as they would like. They, too, may doubt their election and fear reprobation.

It is true that God is a holy God. People who completely give themselves over to an immoral and ungodly life should rightly fear God's wrath. However, there are also those who are saddened by their sins and who are frustrated that their faith and their ability to resist temptation are still so feeble. When God's children go through such struggles, they need not be afraid that they are reprobate. "God has promised not to quench the smoking flax nor to break the bruised reed" (CoD 1.16; see also Isa 42:3; Matt 12:20). All of God's promises, including this one, are "Yes" and "Amen" in Jesus Christ (2 Cor 1:20), to praise of his glory and to the comfort of his people.

COVENANT AND ELECTION

There is one last question concerning election that we touched on earlier but needs extra attention. It revolves around this question: how is God's covenant related to God's election? Are they the same thing? Are they different? If so, how are they different? These questions become practical and personal as well. Should we think of every person who has been baptized, and who so has received the sign of God's covenant, as being one of God's elect?

To begin with, there are lines of similarity between covenant and election. Here are three that can be mentioned briefly:

- The God who initiated the covenant (Gen 17:7) is the same God who made the eternal decree to adopt some sinners as his own children (Eph 1:4).

- God demonstrates his unmerited mercy in the covenant (Deut 7:7–9) just as surely as he shows it in election (Rom 9:15).

- Christ is the mediator of the covenant (Luke 22:20; 1 Tim 2:5), and the decree of election was made in Christ (Eph 1:4–5).

At the same time, election and covenant cannot be equated with each other. There are at least three key differences:

- Election refers to God's plan, or decree, regarding his salvation of sinners (Rom 8:28; Eph 1:5), while the covenant refers to God's relationship with sinners (Lev 26:12).

- God's election occurred before the creation of the world (Eph 1:4), while the covenant was made in time and history with Abraham and his descendants (Gen 17).

- God's decree of election cannot be changed (Ps 33:11), but the covenant can be broken, although it should not be, by sinful human beings (Deut 31:16).

So, how do these two doctrines fit together? Perhaps the most straightforward way is to say that God's covenant of grace is a special instrument that God uses in time and history in order to bring his plan, made before the creation of the world, to completion on the final day. All those whom God chose in eternity will certainly be there, in glory, on the new heaven and earth. Working towards that final goal, God uses the covenant relationship. Not everyone in the covenant of grace is elect, just as "not all who are descended from Israel belong to Israel," as the apostle Paul says in Romans 9:6. Moreover, even though both Jacob and Esau belonged to God's covenant people, and both were circumcised, yet the LORD says, "Jacob I loved, but Esau I hated" (Rom 9:13).

At the same time, even though we know from Scripture that some members of the covenant are not among the elect, this should not send us down into a spiral of spiritual doubt. Instead, let us cling to God's sure promises in faith, repent and flee from all sin, and find our eternal hope in the all-sufficient cross of Christ, the Good Shepherd, who comforts the troubled soul and does not break the bruised reed (Isa 42:3; Matt 12:20; CoD 1.16).

Suggested Readings: Deuteronomy 7:6–11; Ephesians 1:1–14

QUESTIONS FOR UNDERSTANDING

1. You may encounter Christians who speak a lot about choosing for Christ but who know very little about God's electing choice. Briefly but thoroughly, describe how you would introduce this doctrine to them. List at least three essential aspects of this doctrine, and support each aspect with a text from Scripture.

2. Jesus Christ is the cornerstone "rejected by men but in the sight of God chosen and precious" (1 Pet 2:4, 6). Why is it significant that Christ's being chosen was also part of the eternal decree? Also read the Canons of Dort 1.7 and explain what it means that Christ was appointed to be "the Mediator and Head of all the elect"? What is the difference between his role as Mediator and his function as Head? How does each one benefit us?

3. The title of this chapter is "Election: God's Decision to Adopt." Explain what this means. Explore how it helps us understand the doctrine of election more deeply as well as answer some objections that are raised against this doctrine. In addition to Ephesians 1:4–5, the following will be helpful: Romans 8:12–17 (about adoption) and Romans 8:28–39 (about election). Notice especially Romans 8:29, where we read that God's chosen ones are "predestined to be conformed to the image of his Son."

4. What exactly is election on the basis of foreseen faith? Is it just a slightly different opinion about election, or is it a serious error?

QUESTIONS FOR FURTHER DISCUSSION

1. The introduction to this chapter outlines some of the common questions and objections that people have concerning election. Have you heard other questions or objections? If so, what are they, and how would you answer them?

2. Imagine that a fellow member of the church comes to you for advice. She is very worried. Even though she desires with all her heart to be saved, she is afraid that she might be condemned along with the reprobates. How would you guide and comfort her?

3. In the Canons of Dort parents receive the assurance that they ought not to doubt the election and salvation of their covenant children "whom God calls out of this life in their infancy" (CoD 1.17). For how long, or until what age, does this assurance apply? Does this truth also extend to young children? To teenagers? To make this practical, consider the following situation. The sixteen-year-old son of believing parents has died in a car crash. During the last two years he questioned many things about God and faith. He still attended church, but privately his parents used to wonder whether he would continue to worship the Lord if they gave him the option of doing whatever he wanted to on the Lord's Day. What should we say to these parents? Can we say that they, too, ought not to doubt the salvation and election of their child?

COMBINED INDEX

church discipline

    and Lord's supper, 3.152–53

    as mark of the church, 3.48–50

conditional immortality. *See* annihilationism

conversion, 2.134. *See* repentance

covenant, 1.125–36

    and baptism, 3.136–38

    definition of, 1.126–29

    and election, 1.152–54

    in Paradise, 1.133–36

    of works, 1.33–36

    relationship of old and new, 1.131–33

    two parts of, 1.129–31

creation, 1.72–83

    angels, 1.79

    by God the Father, 1.73–76

    and evolution, 1.81–83

    in six days, 1.80–81

    out of nothing (*ex nihilo*), 1.76–77

creeds, 1.3

cremation, 3.183–84

D

deacons, 3.66–67

death, 3.173

    and the body, 3.180–84

    of Christ, 2.39–42

    and the soul, 3.184–87

deification, 3.172

demons, 1.79

descent into hell, 2.43–46

dispensationalism, 1.133, 3.30

Docetism, 2.12–13

doctrine, 1.1–2, 1.8–10

    definition of, 1.4–5

    source of, 1.6–8

dogma, 1.5

dogmatics, 1.3

E

ecclesiology, 3.2–4

elders, 3.64–65

election, 1.139–54, 2.190–91

    and adoption, 1.146–47

    and baptism, 3.136–38

    and covenant, 1.152–54

    definition of, 1.147–49

    not exceeding limits of Scripture, 1.143–47

    on the basis of foreseen faith, 1.150

    scriptural proof for, 1.141–43

environmentalism, 1.109–10

eschatology, 3.162–76, 3.178–93, 3.196–217

    brief survey of events, 3.198–200

    general and personal, 3.178–79, 3.197

    and hermeneutics, 3.174–76

    theocentric approach to, 3.164–68, 3.202–5

eternal glory, 3.215–17

eternal punishment, 3.213–15

eternal state, 3.197–98

Eutyches, 2.12

evangelist, 3.68

evolution, 1.81–83, 3.171–72

F

G

H

9 780099 480590 4